THE
RESILIENCE
PROJECT

Hugh van Cuylenburg has been working in education for more than 17 years, teaching both primary and secondary in a range of educational settings. He has completed post-graduate studies looking at resilience and wellbeing, and has developed and facilitated programs for more than a thousand schools Australia-wide.

In 2015, the National Rugby League asked Hugh to design and implement a series of comprehensive workshops at every single club in the competition. Since then, he has worked with the Australian cricket team, the Australian netball team, the Australian women's soccer team, the Australian women's rugby league team, ten AFL teams, the Australian Olympic Committee and every soccer team in the A-League. Beyond the team environment, Hugh has worked one-on-one with individuals such as Steve Smith, Billy Slater and Dustin Martin.

Outside of schools and elite sport, Hugh has presented to hundreds of corporate organisations as a keynote speaker, and for three years running his national speaking tour has sold out. He is also co-host of the popular podcast *The Imperfects*.

THE

RESILIENCE PROJECT

FINDING HAPPINESS THROUGH GRATITUDE EMPATHY & MINDFULNESS

HUGH VAN CUYLENBURG

LIFE

PENGUIN LIFE

UK | USA | Canada | Ireland | Australia
India | New Zealand | South Africa | China

Penguin Life is part of the Penguin Random House group of companies whose
addresses can be found at global.penguinrandomhouse.com.

Penguin
Random House
Australia

First published by Ebury Press in 2019
This edition published by Penguin Life in 2020

Author photograph on back cover © Tim Caraffa
Cover design by Alex Ross © Penguin Random House Australia Pty Ltd
Typeset in Adobe Garamond by Midland Typesetters, Australia

Printed and bound in Australia by Griffin Press, an accredited
ISO AS/NZS 14001 Environmental Management Systems printer

 A catalogue record for this
book is available from the
NATIONAL
LIBRARY National Library of Australia
OF AUSTRALIA

ISBN 978 1 76089 277 7

penguin.com.au

For my little sister, Georgia.

I am sorry I was unable to protect you, and that I wasn't there for you years later when you needed me most.

I hope this book helps you to understand how much I love you.

CONTENTS

AUTHOR'S NOTE

When I was first approached to write a book, my answer was no. I thought only people of great importance penned books. Who was I to write one?! But when I told my wife Penny, she said, 'Don't be so selfish. People will benefit from your stories, and if it helps to turn one person's life around, it'll be worth it.'

I'm not very good at saying no to Penny.

The Resilience Project: Finding Happiness Through Gratitude, Empathy and Mindfulness is a collection of personal stories that helps to explore the concepts of gratitude, empathy and mindfulness, how you practise them, and the benefits of integrating them into your everyday life.

I am not a psychologist, I am not a psychiatrist and I definitely do not see myself as a motivational speaker. I am a proud teacher and a storyteller.

A warning: this book contains stories about mental

illness, sexual abuse and suicide that may be triggering for some readers. For this reason crisis support services are listed at the back of the book, and I would encourage anyone experiencing mental health issues to contact a GP or mental health practitioner.

Thank you for taking the time to read this book. I hope you find it helpful.

With gratitude,
Hugh van Cuylenburg

CHAPTER 1

THE MOMENT
EVERYTHING CHANGED

Whenever things went wrong in our little corner of the world, Mum would always get busy in the kitchen. Hassles at school? Lasagne. A humbling loss at cricket? Roast chicken. Trouble with girlfriends? Amazing curry. At the first sniff of trouble the house would overflow with heartening aromas as Mum did her best to cook us out of the doldrums.

Dinnertime at the van Cuylenburgs' was the best. Whether we had issues to sort through or not, when I sat down each night with Mum and Dad, my sister Georgia and our little brother Josh, the meals were seasoned with hilarious stories and garnished with joy. For the first 16 years of my life, dinnertime was without doubt the highlight of my day.

Then, in 1996, it suddenly wasn't anymore. A shadow fell across our family, and no amount of Mum's great cooking could make it go away. Georgia was 14 when she stopped eating regular meals. Almost overnight the laughing and the stories ceased. Dinnertime became the worst part of the day. For all of us.

I was only a teenager, and I reacted to the about-face in our family's happy routine by getting frustrated with Georgia and how upset she was making Mum and Dad by refusing to eat. Georgia seemed to have a million excuses about why she couldn't eat this or that type of food. To me, it was infuriating.

Up until then we had been an extraordinarily tight family. We never argued. We never fought. I was close to both my brother and sister, and the three of us worshipped the ground our parents walked on. The worst family disagreement before Georgia's illness was the time Josh – who is six years my junior – hurled a tennis ball into my back. We don't recall what caused the angry outburst, only that Josh cried for the next half-hour because he felt so bad about what he'd done.

But now, daily arguments erupted over food and bubbled over into noisy fights that only grew more and more heated.

Mum would be reduced to tears and soon Dad would start crying, too. I'd sit there at the table in silent disbelief, thinking, 'What is going on here? Georgia – just eat your food, and Mum and Dad will stop crying! Can't you see you're breaking their hearts?'

I'd look helplessly at Josh, who was just 11 – a pretty vulnerable age to see the safety net of your family unravel before your eyes. But then things got even worse. There were arguments about what Georgia ate at school, fights about what was left in her lunchbox when she got home and daily clashes about breakfast. Things got weird; I'd hear arguments erupt at two o'clock in the morning because my parents had found Georgia standing in the pantry, picking the sultanas out of a box of Just Right.

One day Mum and Dad came home from a visit to a doctor and explained anorexia nervosa to me. Or at least, they tried to. 'Your sister is not well, Hugh,' they said. 'She can't help that she doesn't want to eat. You have to understand that it's a mental illness, OK?'

I nodded and mumbled something affirmative, but the truth was I didn't understand it at all. 'It's an illness? Don't be ridiculous,' I thought to myself. 'If she eats food she'll get better and our family will be happy again and Mum and Dad won't be crying, so why won't she just fucking eat?'

As I stuffed my head deeper into the sand, anorexia started to show physically on Georgia. She ceased to resemble my little sister; she became a gaunt, pallid stick figure in a nightie, thinning hair matted across her face as she fluttered weakly to the pantry in the middle of the night, like an emaciated moth to a barely flickering flame.

'Georgia!' I said, when I interrupted one of her 2 am missions. 'Get back to bed!' But she just looked at me as if I wasn't there, and slowly returned to the box of Just Right and her micro-feast of hardened sultana fragments.

I thought things couldn't get any more distressing, but they did. Georgia's efforts in the kitchen went from bizarre to near toxic. She would slather Brussels sprouts in balsamic vinegar and microwave them on high for three minutes. She'd read somewhere that if you nuke sprouts and balsamic vinegar for long enough there'll be no calories left, rendering the meal acceptable for her consumption. The house stank of burnt sprouts for a year.

It wasn't only Georgia's diet and appearance that became scary. When I returned from school one afternoon I had to pick my way through shards of glass to get inside. Georgia had made a border for her bedroom mirror using pictures of girls in bikinis she'd cut out from magazines. She'd then wrapped the mirror up in a blanket, carried it outside and stomped all over it. The glass went everywhere but Georgia tried to explain to us that it was a way of smashing her bad thoughts. 'So they won't beat me this time,' she said.

Georgia justified all of her behaviour – no matter how extreme – and she argued passionately that it was the right thing to do. The relentless madness of it did my teenage head in. I couldn't process what was happening to her and what it was doing to my family, so I eventually turned my back on the situation.

In Year 12 I had a girlfriend I was madly in love with. Her name was Christie, and she was from a very happy family who lived on hundreds of acres of land on the out-skirts of Melbourne. I spent as much time there as I could, around three or four nights a week. In hindsight it amounted to abandonment; I left my sister, my little brother and my poor Mum and Dad to deal with anorexia's daily torment by themselves.

Even though I understood mental illness on an intellec-tual level (sort of), I would still silently scoff about it and implore Georgia to just eat food. I'd get angry whenever I'd hear about people with cancer, knowing there was nothing *they* could do to get better. The way I saw it, our family's problems had an easy fix. 'If it's an illness where you don't eat, all you have to do is eat and you'll get better!'

Every Tuesday we'd go to family counselling sessions to try to navigate a way through our living hell. I couldn't help but take the piss out of these sessions in the lift down from the office afterwards. Deep down, however, I was resentful because the counsellor would say things like, 'Hugh, do you understand the role you play in your sister's recovery?' I'd sit there and think, 'You're kidding, aren't you? If my sister eats, she gets better. Don't talk about my role in this because there's a very simple solution.'

I was blinded by the arrogance of youth. The counsellor was only trying to help us but I felt as though she was pointing the finger at me, even though she wasn't. At any rate, the family therapy didn't seem to get us anywhere.

I was so worn out by the constant misery at home that whenever I was there I'd try to lighten the mood. While Mum cooked in times of trouble, my instinct was to tell funny stories. I desperately wanted us to be a happy family again so I'd sit at the dinner table and tell wildly embellished stories about my day. One night I found myself short of material, so when it was time for dinner I walked into the dining room completely nude and pulled up a chair as if nothing was up: 'Righto, what's for dinner?' Anything for laughter instead of tears. Anything to try to make my family a bit happier.

Sadly I continued to dismiss anorexia as something that Georgia, for whatever reason, had decided she wanted to inflict on herself and the rest of us. By the time I truly understood she was at the mercy of a mental illness and had no more control over her suffering than a cancer patient has over tumours, it was almost too late.

Georgia was 17 when she was admitted to hospital in the school holidays before she started Year 12. She'd fronted up to her weekly weigh-in and registered below her crisis weight of 34 kilograms. Into an eating disorders unit at Austin Hospital she went.

When I saw the full spectrum of medical science deployed to keep my little sister from starving to death, it finally registered: 'She's sick. She needs help.' Georgia was ringed by doctors, nurses, psychiatrists and orderlies, and a gutted family who tried not to weep too much at her bedside. She was so weak she could barely move.

Each day the medicos limited the time we could spend with Georgia; it was a way of providing an incentive to eat. The deal was that if she put on some weight we could stay longer than the set period, but if she didn't we'd have to go.

When we left the hospital on the first day, Mum, Dad, Josh and I moped back across a footbridge to where the car was parked. I couldn't bring myself to walk alongside them though; I was ashamed. I strode ten metres ahead, bawling my eyes out because I realised I hadn't been supportive to them, I hadn't been there enough and – worst of all – I hadn't recognised the legitimacy of Georgia's suffering. But I sure understood it now. 'She can't help this,' I cried to myself. 'She doesn't want to be in hospital. She doesn't want us to be upset. Georgia doesn't want to die!'

The doctor had been pretty blunt with me. 'It's serious,' he'd said on that first afternoon. 'This could be it for your sister. That's why she's in here.' If it had simply been a matter of Georgia eating a sandwich and – boom! – we'd be a happy family again, then she would have done it years ago. Instead she was now sentenced to suffer without us.

Georgia shared the ward with three other girls who were also battling anorexia. One day an awful stench permeated the room, but the hospital staff couldn't work out what was causing it or where it was coming from. It turned out the girl in the bed next to Georgia's had figured out a way to rort the system. She would say to the nurses, 'OK, I'll eat the dinner but not in front of anyone else. You have to close the curtain.' Safe from prying eyes, she would dismantle the swivel-around TV set that hung above her bed, stuff whatever food she'd been given into the back and close it up again. When the curtains were pulled back she'd say: 'Look, I've eaten!' The penny dropped a week later when nurses finally traced the source of the smell. The lengths these girls went to in order to prevent weight gain were extraordinary, and a constant reminder that when mental illness takes hold, the control it can have over someone is terrifying.

By the time I was 21 years old, Georgia had been sick for four years. During that time I had grown very good at compartmentalising problems. I was quite adept at putting anorexia aside and telling myself, 'You've got your relationship. You've got your mates. Life is great!'

In hospital with a dying little sister, though, it dawned on me that human beings are not made up of compartments. 'Oh my God,' I thought to myself. 'What have you been doing for the past four years?'

I suddenly had empathy for Georgia, even though it had taken a life-or-death crisis for me to see things from her point of view. There was nothing I could have done to stop anorexia gnawing away at Georgia, and nothing more my parents could have done either, but I could have been there a hell of a lot more. I had chosen to disconnect at a time when family connections were vital.

From then on, I vowed to always try to see things from

other people's perspectives, and to do my best to help those in need.

Ever since she was a little girl Georgia had been larger than life. She was bright, funny, energetic and she was always, *always* performing. Her presence alone demanded attention. When I was in Year 2 Georgia started in prep at the same primary school, but after just a few weeks Mum noticed I was a little sullen.

'Are you OK, Hugh?' she asked me one day after school. 'Is everything alright?'

Apparently I replied, in a defeated tone, 'Oh Mum, Georgia's everywhere!'

I loved my sport but I was a pretty shy kid who tried to fly under the radar – a tall order when I had Georgia as my trusty sidekick. Whenever we'd go to the park she would walk straight up to any other kids who happened to be there and lay down the law: 'OK, everyone, just so you know my brother is here and he's got superpowers. So don't mess with us, alright?'

Naturally the kids would demand I demonstrate these supernatural abilities on the spot, so I'd have to explain that I didn't have any; I was a mere mortal who just wanted to play on the swings. But Georgia would have none of it. 'Just show them, Hugh!' she'd say. 'Show them what you can do!'

At primary school Georgia was better friends with many more people than I was – even kids in the higher grades who I hadn't met before. It was the same deal when she joined me in high school at Carey Baptist Grammar School. Georgia exploded onto the scene in Year 7. She knew just about everyone and even dated guys from the grades above mine – boys in the senior school, which I found odd and a bit embarrassing. Georgia *was* everywhere.

Then, seemingly overnight, she'd got sick and everything had changed. Georgia's stint in Austin Hospital lasted two weeks but it felt like two years. I can't imagine how bad it must have been for her. We'd visit her every day and, gradually, Georgia fought her way back to us by putting on enough weight to be deemed 'well' enough to go home.

Despite missing nearly the first month of Year 12 and although she'd struggle to free herself from anorexia's grip for years after, Georgia managed to graduate from high school with an ENTER score (the equivalent of the current-day ATAR) of 96.40. It was streets ahead of what I'd managed three years earlier. That achievement was testimony not only to Georgia's intelligence but also to her fierce, unstoppable drive.

At university she went even harder. Georgia studied public relations at RMIT University and graduated with ridiculously high marks. She was so focused that she used to sticky-tape her research notes on the steering wheel, rear-vision mirror and the dash of her car, so whenever she was stopped at the lights or stuck in traffic she could cram in more study.

In 2004 Georgia moved to Los Angeles to pursue a career as an actor, and has lived there ever since. Nowadays she's an American citizen and to say that she is flourishing is an understatement.

About five years ago, however, Mum and Dad phoned Josh and me out of the blue. 'Georgia's coming home,' they said. 'She needs to talk to us all about something that's pretty urgent, so you need to be here tomorrow night.'

The following evening we all assembled at Mum and Dad's house, unsure of what to expect. 'So, I've been getting therapy and counselling for the anorexia,' Georgia began. 'My counsellors are always saying to me, "Has something happened to you in your past? Has something traumatic happened that has caused all this?" And I always tell them, "No. Nothing of the sort. I had a great childhood."'

The counsellors were also curious about Georgia's choice of men. Ever since she was young, she had a pattern of dating guys a lot older than her. There were the boys in the senior grades she'd dated while she was in Year 7 and 8, and in her mid-twenties she was with men in their fifties.

'So the counsellors have asked, "Has your father done something to you?" And of course I say, "No, definitely not."' Georgia smiled reassuringly at Dad.

'But they press on: "What about uncles? Grandparents? Old family friends?"'

But Georgia said she was always adamant: 'No. All the men in my family are wonderful, caring and gentle people who have never harmed me.'

As Georgia explained this to us, I wondered where it was all heading. Finally she came to the point. 'The thing is,' she said, 'I had a nightmare the other night and it was about what happened to me when we were in Sydney.'

Georgia took a deep breath and continued. 'I would have been about three years old, and we were in the front garden at Grandma and Grandpa's house. Mum and Dad had a rule that if we played in the front garden we had to play in front of the window where they could see us . . .'

My blood ran ice cold. As soon as she said those words I felt like I was suddenly a child again, and I had a strong idea of what might be coming.

I remembered those instructions about playing in front

of the window at Mum's parents' place on Sydney's North Shore. Being the firstborn and a somewhat responsible six-year-old, I obeyed the rules, but being a spirited three-year-old, Georgia had absent-mindedly drifted out of Mum and Dad's designated field of vision.

While we were playing, a man who would have been in his fifties or sixties walked into the yard. I can't remember his exact words but he spoke to me first and said something like, 'I'm friends with your dad. Come over here, I want to show you something.'

I declined to go to him so he walked over to where Georgia was playing, picked her up in a very familiar way and said something like, 'I've got something to show you. Do you want to see it?'

His manner was so relaxed and so familiar that I didn't think anything of it. My six-year-old mind figured that he must have been one of Dad's friends, just like he'd said he was. But here was Georgia, a quarter of a century later, about to tell us what happened next.

'A man came into the yard, picked me up and took me around the side of the house, where he sexually assaulted me,' Georgia said.

This hurt had been buried so deep down in Georgia's psyche that it only came to the surface in a nightmare half a lifetime later. 'I woke up crying and I knew it wasn't a dream,' Georgia continued. 'I knew straight away that it actually happened to me. All this time counsellors and psychologists have been trying to find out what happened to me, and that was it.'

After that traumatic experience, Georgia had become the biggest stickler for the rules, and had tied herself in knots trying to be the very best she could. She strived to be perfect for Mum and Dad because she didn't dare make another mistake. It was as if she had spent the rest of her life being careful to never stray outside the view from Grandma and Grandpa's window. That mindset helps to explain why the obsessive rules she gave herself about eating – or not eating – were so rigid.

Just as sinister and insidious were the words Georgia says her attacker spoke before he left: 'If you tell anyone about this, your parents won't love you or want you anymore.' What an evil, despicable thing to say, and what a horrible thought to make a child carry for the rest of her life. Though I try not to dwell on it too much, I look back on this memory with immense sadness, and I mourn the loss of potential in my relationship with Georgia. In hindsight, what I came to see as her increased need for competition with me, aiming to look as perfect as possible in Mum and Dad's eyes, was a response to the events of that horrific day. Georgia is such an amazing person but I can't help wondering how our relationship would have turned out if that hadn't happened to her. It's depressing and heartbreaking to think a human being can wander into a sunny garden, defile a child and walk away, oblivious and unburdened by the human wreckage he has left behind.

I now understand why my sister had wished I had superpowers when we were kids.

Our family suffered, like countless others who have been scarred by heinous crimes and struggled under the pressure of mental illnesses.

Of course, mental illness is extraordinarily complex and I don't want to suggest that there's a clear-cut cause for it as in my sister's case. But when I reflect on it all, I realise that ever since Georgia was diagnosed with anorexia, I have been fascinated with the question: what makes people happy? Back in 1996, my concern was more with my immediate family's happiness: I knew that I had no control over Georgia's mental illness, and that she was in the capable hands of doctors and psychiatrists, but I wanted to make my mum and dad happy again, and I wanted to allow my little brother to enjoy the same carefree childhood years that I did.

With the clarity of hindsight, and taking into account all of my sister's extraordinary achievements in life, I now realise that just as Georgia's torment became a part of my family's story, it has also been woven into a new story, not just for her and for the van Cuylenburgs but for families throughout the country – one of vulnerability, hope and resilience.

CHAPTER 2
A LESSON IN GRATITUDE

I was destined to come into the world off the long run. As a descendant of a line of cricket tragics, I have the game in my DNA. My grandfather was a gifted cricketer, and my dad enjoyed a successful career in grade cricket, ascending to the role of captain–coach of Melbourne University Cricket Club (MUCC). From my standpoint, though, the most important games Dad ever played were fought out in our backyard.

By the time I was old enough to properly hold a bat in the mid-'80s, that backyard in the Melbourne suburb of Balwyn was my spiritual home and the centre of my ever-expanding cricket universe. If Mum and Dad were busy I'd be out there on my own, bowling at the stumps nonstop. I wasn't the greatest batsman in Balwyn, but I *loved* bowling.

Although I played alone a lot, I was never short of imaginary teammates and a feisty opposition to do battle with. I cast myself as Australia's strike bowler in the tense, extremely serious international clashes I concocted inside my head. I never got too cocky or fantasised that I bowled England out for 40 runs or took ten wickets in every innings; my games were fair, realistic and considered, and they lasted all afternoon, with me bowling methodically at the stumps. England would usually score around 230 runs but I would take five or six wickets, and there was always an exceptional spell to reflect on later.

Dad bought me a plastic cricket ball that had a pretty big seam to enable swing. I knew from a young age I was able to bowl really nice left-arm inswingers, just like Dad said Grandpa had done. I'd aim to bring the ball back at the top of off-stump and I'd get pretty excited when I succeeded, but not half as excited as commentator Bill Lawry would be inside my head: *'Got him! Yeeessss! The young Victorian has struck again, knocking off-stump out of the ground with a massive inswinger!'*

Sometimes I'd bowl bouncers and sledge the pretend batsmen, and Bill would remark on how competitive I was. If I could convince Dad to join me, which wasn't usually that hard, we'd play a game where we'd face 20 balls each over two innings. We could run between the wickets and score boundaries by hitting the different fences. If you got out, you lost three runs off your total.

Mum, a librarian who'd by now had a fair bit to do with cricket, played more of a coaching role. Even though she often had her hands full with us three kids, Mum was the one who actually taught me the mechanics of bowling, because Dad was working pretty hard at his dental practice most of the time. Mum showed me how to keep my arm straight and to brush my ear with it as I rotated through the delivery – all the technical stuff she'd picked up by watching the game.

By the time I was six, cricket was everything to me. My bedroom walls were plastered with McDonald's posters of the Australian side as well as all the touring teams from around the world. I could rattle off the names of every player, and I just knew that one day I was going to represent Australia, too. Mum and Dad only fanned the flames; even as a little boy I was allowed to stay up late to revel in the excitement of day–night matches.

As each summer rolled around, our backyard in Balwyn

became more and more like the Melbourne Cricket Ground in the Panavision of my mind, and the cicadas were transformed into the roaring home crowd. The sun would sear through the gum leaves as I walked to my mark, wiped the sweat off my brow and began my long run-up.

'Afternoon Richie, afternoon all, and welcome back to the MCG! It's all happening here. We're seeing a wonderful spell from the young Australian pace man,' Bill Lawry would observe. *'He's bowling fast, he's swinging the ball and the Sri Lankans are rattled.'*

Dad would curate close finishes in our suburban arena. He'd underarm the ball to me and he knew just where to pitch it so I could score, and just where to pitch it to get me out, so it was easy for him to manufacture a nailbiter. During one memorable clash when I was six or seven, I needed two runs off the last ball to win.

'There's a lot of pressure on the young Victorian at the crease, Hugh van Cuylenburg,' Bill Lawry pointed out as Dad got ready to underarm the final ball of the match. I glanced around the yard, weighing up my scoring options as the Nine Network's imaginary cameras beamed me into millions of homes around the country.

'Two runs needed for victory. It's all happening here, as the Sri Lankan quick comes running in to bowl . . .'

Dad pitched up a juicy half-volley; he had clearly decided to give me the opportunity to win. I managed to whack the ball into a gap between two gum trees, definitely enough to allow me to run two and win the game.

'Whoa! He's got a hold of that . . .'

I scampered up the yard and turned, but as I was coming back for the second run I saw Dad had picked up the ball. His competitive nature must have kicked in, because he had a shot at the stumps from miles away, between the narrow gap in the trees. It hit! I was spectacularly run out, just one run shy of victory. Frustrated and upset, I hurled my bat hard into the wood paling fence and burst into tears.

Bill Lawry fell silent as Dad slowly walked over to where I was sobbing on the grass. He got down on his haunches, looked me in the eye and said very calmly and very clearly: 'Don't you ever behave like that. If you carry on like that again, it will be the last game of cricket we ever play together.'

I was stunned. Dad had never spoken to me in that way before. I don't think he has since. It's not as if he raised his voice or was visibly angry; there was just something profound about what he said and how he said it. I understood immediately I was being given an important life lesson.

From that moment I knew it really matters how you

behave when things don't go your way, and I adjusted my attitude accordingly. Even during spirited lunchtime games of cricket at Greythorn Primary School, I made sure I never again showed disappointment or carried on like a brat if I got out or lost a game.

Though Dad didn't say it in so many words, there was more to his message than simply not being a dickhead: he was also saying that having the opportunity to play cricket was more than enough to celebrate. Being able-bodied, having someone to play with, having a dad, owning a bat and a ball and having somewhere to play – those were victories in life, and they counted more than the tally on the scoreboard ever could.

Twenty years later I would receive a lesson in gratitude again, not from Dad or another wise elder, but from an underprivileged boy who also loved his cricket.

More than anything else in my life, I have defined myself through sport in general and cricket in particular. I excelled right through primary school and into Carey Baptist Grammar, where I captained the cricket team and the athletics team. On weekends I played grade cricket for the Prahran Cricket Club, just like Dad had done. I loved sport and I felt as though it loved me right back; my child-hood successes were an assurance that I was indeed destined to play for Australia and take my place on the bedroom walls of other starry-eyed children.

Right on cue, in Year 12 the Victorian Institute of Sport took notice of my bowling and awarded me a one-year scholarship. I regarded myself as a serious sportsman on the move and I wore my VIS gear everywhere I went – particu-larly if I was feeling insecure.

Though I was very sporty and outgoing, deep down I was shy. My shirt with the VIS logo sewn into the collar was an affirmation but it was also armour plating against the hos-tile self-doubt that would occasionally creep in. We are all prone to insecurity and shame in some way. I knew I wasn't an exceptionally good-looking person, and I wasn't the high-est academic achiever, so I clung desperately to my identity as an elite sportsperson. What I recognise now is that when I wore my VIS shirt, I was trying to compensate by project-ing the image of myself as a sportsman destined for first-class cricket. In hindsight, I imagine some people saw me as a first-class wanker.

At 18 I took another step on the road to national selec-tion when I was picked to represent Victoria in the under-19s team at the Australian Cricket Championships in Adelaide.

Suddenly I was up against guys I'd heard about who were *definitely* destined for greatness.

In the semifinal we came up against the New South Wales side, which boasted a young batsman by the name of Michael Clarke. I'd heard a lot about Michael so I knew I was about to find out just how good he was. I was handed the ball early in his innings, as New South Wales set out to chase our total of 180. I steamed in off my long run and fired a full-ish delivery that swung back late and thudded into his pads, plumb in front of the stumps it looked to me.

'Howzaaaat?!' I screamed as my teammates rushed over to congratulate me. I enjoyed a few milliseconds of elation until the umpire delivered his verdict: 'Not out,' he said, shaking his head.

Michael was incredible that day. He went on to score 120, and New South Wales absolutely destroyed us. On the bus back to our accommodation, I remember feeling flat: I had truly come face-to-face with an elite sportsman, and now my own identity as an elite sportsman was coming under challenge. Little did I know that Michael Clarke would eventually retire from international cricket in 2015 with 115 Test matches, 245 One Day Internationals and the Australian captaincy under his belt.

While it was a challenging tour on many levels, though, I felt honoured to even be there playing against these guys, and my time at the tournament remains one of the greatest experiences of my life.

On the flight home, part of me was thinking, 'OK, what am I going to do now?' Throughout my life people had always told me I was a great bowler, so I was a little confused when I found out I wasn't anywhere near fast enough to make it at the top level.

Back in Melbourne I didn't exactly give up on the idea of playing first-class cricket; I just dialled back my expectations. I continued to wear my VIS shirt like an emotional exoskeleton and I kept giving cricket my all. As I began to have more experience with the social side of cricket, it started to dawn on me that it wasn't just a game; cricket was a national institution in which I was able to learn about friendship, sportsmanship, commitment, fairness and how to treat others.

Sometimes the lessons came in the form of a cautionary tale. When I was in my late teens, my captain and coach was a former international player who, two years earlier, had made a century at the MCG. As a batsman he was incredible. As a coach? Not so much. He, too, had detected I wasn't the fastest pace bowler in Victoria, but rather than encourage me he tried to saddle me with the nickname 'Belinda' because he reckoned I bowled slower than the Australian women's cricketer Belinda Clark.

'Are you going to bowl soon, Belinda?' he'd ask derisively when we were in the field.

At the time I read this as an attempt to emasculate me. And it worked a treat: I didn't feel good about myself and, as a result, I didn't bowl well. I soon realised this was the captain's overarching approach to 'leadership' – to bully and belittle all the guys in the team in the insecure belief that it would lift our performance. It was largely because of him that I vowed if I ever got the opportunity to captain or coach a team I would go the opposite route: I would love and embrace every single person in my side – not just the players, but also the volunteers and supporters. I would focus on their strengths; nurture, support and encourage them; and pump them up at every opportunity. And I vowed never to disparage female cricketers.

I'd always thought cricket gave me a strong work ethic in the sense that I knew the only way to get a task done properly was through practice and dedication. I'd applied myself in a similar way at school, too; I'd taken it seriously and studied hard. Beyond that my only experience of work came through my part-time job selling movie tickets and choc-tops at Palace Balwyn Cinema.

With its art-deco facade, warm lighting and the reassuring smell of popcorn forever hanging in the climate-controlled air, working in the cinema wasn't exactly like descending into a coalmine. It was the cosiest job in Australia. I might not have been the most punctual or well-presented employee in the history of the cinema complex, but I did go to great lengths to ensure patrons had a wonderful experience if I was the one who happened to be serving them on the night. Some nights, though, business was so quiet in Balwyn it was all I could do to stay awake.

During one night shift I got so bored and hungry I let myself into the storeroom, an off-limits treasure trove of chips, chocolates and lollies for the candy bar. I flicked the lights on, looked around at the shelves full of booty, hesitated for a moment then selected a box of Cheezels. I peeled open the silver pillow full of crunchy rings and pushed a few into my mouth. I knew it was the wrong thing to do, but I thought, 'What's one packet of Cheezels in the grand scheme of things?'

After munching through a quarter of the box, I started to worry that the light would draw the attention of the cinema manager. I quickly flipped the switch again and settled onto the floor of the storeroom to finish my ill-gotten snack in pitch darkness. As I neared the end of the box, I threaded Cheezels onto every finger of both hands and proceeded to remove them whole, one delicious snack at a time. At the very moment my index finger and its passenger were disappearing into my wide-open mouth, the door flung open, the light flicked on, and in burst the manager, catching me orange-handed. Despite how hard I tried, it was difficult to pull an innocent face. It's fair to say that landed me in a bit of strife.

A few years later I thought back to the bliss of Balwyn Cinema as I hunched over in a freezing, muddy pit near Heathrow Airport and shovelled rubble into an excavator bucket. At the age of 20 I was offered an opportunity to play cricket professionally in England, at the club of Finchampstead in Berkshire. Although the standard wasn't as good as I'd hoped, it was still adequate and I took the game seriously.

I was given six months' free board in a beautiful home owned by the club's chairman and paid to train and play in the Thames Valley Premier League. The chairman was an eccentric old bachelor who was often out of town on business so, with not much else to do during the week, I figured

I should get a job. The club was kind enough to line me up with a position labouring for a company that was laying new gas pipes at Heathrow.

I'd get picked up by a crew in a big van at 5.30 am and driven to the worksite, where I spent 12 hours a day on the end of a shovel in the bottom of a trench, scooping up the crumbs of dirt and rock that the excavators had missed. Nine days out of ten it was raining and windy.

In addition to the tough conditions, I was easy pickings for the other workers on the job. I'd arrived in England with a nice suntan and for some reason – like a lot of Australian cricketers of the day (I'm looking at you, Michael Clarke) – I had deemed it necessary to bleach my hair peroxide-blond. To the average Brit, the hairdo was a flashing neon sign that said: 'I'm an Aussie! Unleash hell!'

And boy did I cop it. The very first morning, as I climbed into the truck, the bloke sitting next to me said, 'Good morning, tosser!'

'What did you just call me?'

'Look at you. Only a tosser walks around with hair like that.'

Sure enough, my nickname stuck: Tosser. As soon as I'd climb into the van of a morning, several English lads would pile on me about how physically weak I was, how soft I was, how terrible Aussies were in general and how I was the worst worker they'd ever had. And yet I'd sit there, copping it on the chin, and think to myself, 'How good is this?' After a lifetime of comfort, of private schools, living at home with my parents and spending my formative years 'working' at Balwyn Cinema, I badly needed a dose of reality. Although my co-workers could be brutal, they were a brilliant group of people when it came down to it. It took me a while to realise that their bullying was a twisted form of affection, and was sometimes feedback that I desperately needed to hear at that stage in my life.

If labouring in England was a great way to harden me up, playing cricket there was a great way to soften my rigid approach to the game. I'd never been too much of a drinker but in Finchampstead, where the only pub in the village happened to be at the cricket club, most of the players loved a beer. On summer nights in England it often doesn't get dark until 9.30, so we'd stand around having a pint or two, then do a bit of cricket training, then have another pint.

That was all well and good for training, but when it came time to represent the club in competition I took it as seriously as I did when representing Victoria in the under-19s. After all, I was being paid to perform. During one early match we bowled first and went back in the changing rooms to get ready to go out and bat. With ten minutes left before he was due to walk back onto the oval, one of our opening batsmen ambled over and sat down next to me with his pads on, his bat in one hand and a pint of lager in the other. I couldn't believe what I was seeing.

'What . . . what are you doing?' I said incredulously.

'What do you mean?' He sounded genuinely puzzled.

'Are you drinking?'

'I'm having a pint,' he agreed, nodding.

'You're meant to go out and bat in a minute!'

'And?'

'Well, what the fuck are you doing?' I couldn't get over his attitude, and I wouldn't let it go.

A couple of other players wandered over. One of them chimed in: 'I'm heading to the bar. Do you want a pint, Hugh?'

'Yeah, have a drink. Relax,' the beer-sipping batsman followed up. 'You're taking cricket way too seriously. It's just a game.'

'You won't bat as well if you have that. Is that what you want?'

A voice called out from the other side of the dressing room, followed by several more: 'We don't care, mate. Just have a beer.'

It took me a long time to heed the advice. By the last few games of the season I started to relax, and it was great. I wished I'd been able to do it sooner. Cricket training became a laid-back ritual of hitting the nets for half an hour, then walking 50 metres to the pub to chat and watch everyone else train, before rejoining the session when you'd finished your beer. I looked forward to cricket as much for the friendship as the sport.

To make training even more interesting we invented some ridiculous games, including a pastime called Super-Extreme Eyeball Cricket. We'd feed tennis balls into the mechanical bowling machine, set it to 100 kilometres an hour and take turns trying to swat the balls away with a bat before they hit us and left a nasty welt. The first time we played, I refused to wear a helmet. 'It's only a tennis ball!' I sneered. Twenty seconds later I was struck in the left eye. I had never seen grown men laugh so hard. I couldn't see for half an hour afterwards and my eye swelled up to what seemed like the size of an orange. Hence the name Super-Extreme Eyeball Cricket.

Later that year I returned to Australia slightly older, a good deal worldlier and definitely more relaxed about my attitude to cricket. I'd accepted that I wasn't ever going to wear the baggy green or compete at the highest level, but my love of the sport and the camaraderie that goes with it has never since dimmed.

Once again I followed in Dad's footsteps. I left Prahran Cricket Club and joined MUCC at the age of 22. Aside from the sepia-toned memories of the backyard in Balwyn, Melbourne University truly became my cricketing spiritual home. Many of my closest friendships have come through the club, and in 2006 – 30 years after Dad held the position – I became coach. I reckon Grandpa would have been proud.

Sometimes people ask what I love about cricket. Well, it's the hot mornings and long, long summer days in the field with ten people who you've grown close with. It's having a common goal, it's the smell of grass clippings, the fear of fast bowlers and the fear of failure. It's fierce competition with the opposition and it's chatting to them afterwards and becoming mates. It's sweating, it's being a young talent then not being a young talent. It's Super-Extreme Eyeball Cricket. It's the smell of sunscreen. It's watching young, talented players come through, nurturing them and seeing them fall in love with the game the same way I did. It's beers after the game. It's looking forward to training on Tuesday and Thursday nights. It's learning to lose well. It's the feeling of taking a wicket, of bettering the batsmen and nearly being crushed by your bear-hugging teammates.

It's everything, but it's still just a game.

These days I'm no longer coaching; I'm happy to play the role of number-one ticket holder at the club and watch the younger guys come through. I don't mind for a moment that I never made it to the top in cricket, because if I had I probably wouldn't have found my true purpose in life: to help as many people as possible be as happy as they can be.

CHAPTER 3
FINDING PURPOSE

Now that it was settled I wouldn't be playing cricket for a living, I had to figure out what to do with the rest of my life. Being hopelessly sports-obsessed, I wondered if I might instead be a physiotherapist or a sports psychologist so I could at least work alongside elite athletes. Deep down, though, my heart wasn't in it.

After returning from England I did some serious soul-searching. I looked back over my life and asked myself what was important. What did I honestly care most about? Part of me – the little Hugh clutching a rubber ball in the backyard – kept saying, 'It's cricket! It's cricket for sure!' But another inner voice spoke up much more clearly; it belonged to the maturing young adult Hugh, who was still scarred and haunted by the emotional rigours that mental illness had subjected his family to.

'I want to make sure no other families go through what we – and what Georgia – went through,' I found myself thinking over and over as I tried to map out my future. 'If I could stop even one family experiencing what we did, then that would be an achievement in life and a goal worth pursuing.'

I decided that being a teacher was the most direct route. At the very least I'd have 30 kids to look after between 9 am and 3.30 pm, five days a week. And that was it – my entire plan for freeing the world from mental illness, right there. 'Just get in a position where you're working alongside children,' I thought. 'Then at least you'll be there to help if and when they have problems.'

I had no strategy for how I was going to stop students developing mental illnesses or how I'd prevent families suffering the associated trauma. I was pretty naive: I thought that if I was a teacher I could keep a close eye on every kid on my watch. But I had to start somewhere, and as a school-teacher I would at least be at the coalface.

In 2002, I enrolled at Deakin University and completed a Bachelor of Education. As a newly minted young male primary school teacher I was flooded with job opportunities when I graduated, because there weren't too many of us around at the time. There still aren't. I could have taken my pick from a range of positions but I chose to teach at Fintona – an exclusive all-girls school in Melbourne – because I knew anorexia nervosa is more common among young women.

On my first day it was pointed out that I was one of four men on a staff of 80 educators, and the other three men were over the age of 50. I was promptly given a class of Year 5 girls to teach. Year 5 was the most junior level at the Fintona senior campus, which catered to students right through to Year 12.

From the get-go my focus was not only on educating them in literacy and numeracy, but also on elevating and protecting their wellbeing. During my university studies I had gravitated to child and adolescent mental health and pastoral care, and read up on the literature on mental illness. I knew that self-esteem was a huge issue with girls and young women.

I strongly believed – still do – that if we helped to keep the mental and emotional health of students in check then everything else would click for them; maths would become easier, literacy would become easier, studying would become easier and they would socialise better. However, I was a brand-new employee in a hundred-year-old institution that was judged mainly on how well the students did academically, which I totally understood. I went ahead with my more pastoral approach anyway, which involved me putting a focus on listening and engaging emotionally with the students.

I learned a lot about ten- and 11-year-old girls very quickly. How sensitive the kids in my class were, for instance. But also how at that age girls can be brutal. It's as if they've grown claws but they don't yet know how to use them. When they decide to be mean they are a lot crueller than they intend to be.

On my first day, one of the girls raised her hand and asked, 'Why do you have such big eyeballs, Mr V? They're very poppy.' I felt as if I was back in England, on the van to the Heathrow worksite. Though I had come to terms with my lack of good looks, the comment was an invitation for the rest of them to chime in with their thoughts on my appearance.

'And you're going bald, too,' one of the girls said. A few more hands shot up, but I said, 'OK, girls, thank you. I get the point.'

Most hands went down, but one stayed up. 'Oh, I was just going to say you have a really big nose, too.'

Talk about honest feedback!

My students were incredibly creative and talented, and I loved that in the all-girls environment there was no fear of what boys thought of them. They were happy to put their pictures up on the wall and to speak up without the fear of some young lad shooting them down.

Being a 25-year-old man teaching girls aged ten and 11 was always going to have its moments. One of the most awkward arrived pretty early on. The other Year 5 teacher, a lovely young woman, collared me one day and said, 'I don't want to teach sex education, so that's yours.'

'Err, right,' I thought. 'OK . . . um, sex ed with thirty little girls. What could go wrong?'

Well, for the young ladies, it was a chance to create absolute mayhem – the kind of mayhem that occurs when there's a bird in the classroom trying desperately to escape. I thought I was pretty clever when I introduced a question box for the sex ed lesson, but they obviously saw it as their golden opportunity. I left the box out during the week so the girls could ask questions without being embarrassed – and so I could research the hell out of their queries. At the end of the week, I'd answer them.

It worked well during the first week; I studied up on the questions they'd asked and came back with sound answers for them. I felt much more relaxed about sex ed a couple of weeks later, so much so that I didn't bother researching for the lesson. When Friday rolled around I casually announced, 'OK, girls, time for the question box.'

I reached in and pulled out the pieces of paper; there were only three. The first one read: 'Do dogs have periods?'

I didn't have the faintest idea whether dogs had periods or not. I must have missed that lecture at uni. But I wanted to present myself as confident and knowledgeable to the girls, so I read the question out loud to the class: 'This person has asked, "Do dogs have periods?"' I said. 'The answer is no. No, they don't have periods.'

One girl, no doubt the author of the question, put her hand up. 'Um, sir, I think my dog did the other day,' she said. 'There was blood on the floor, on the carpet!'

'Well then,' I said. 'I think it must have cut itself.'

The next question out of the box was, 'What happens if you put your bra on upside down?'

I eyeballed them all, thinking someone was having a lend, but I was met with a sea of straight faces.

'That's a good question. A *good* question,' I said. 'What happens if you put your bra on upside down? I think it would be uncomfortable, wouldn't it? I actually don't know.'

The third and final question was, 'What is a wet dream?'

I rolled my eyes and groaned out loud. I could feel a bead of sweat rolling down my forehead. But this was sex ed. I was the teacher and they wanted an answer.

'Well . . . it's when a person has a dream that they like,' I began.

A hand shot up. 'Why is it called a wet dream though?'

'W-well,' I said, as my mouth started to go dry, 'sometimes they kind of wet the, ah . . . they wet the bed a little bit.'

Another hand slowly floated up. 'Does my dad do this?'

'Oh God,' I thought.

'Yes,' I said evenly. 'Yes, he probably does.'

'Does everyone's dad do this?' she pressed.

'Oh Jesus Christ!' My internal monologue intensified.

'Yes. They all wet the bed, OK?'

'What do you mean they "wet the bed"?' another voice chimed in.

I couldn't wrap it up fast enough. 'Look, they wet the bed,' I said. 'That's it. The end!'

The following Monday I received 20 emails from parents ranging from, 'What on earth are you teaching our children?'

to 'You need to brush up on sex ed' to 'Good thing you're a teacher, not a vet.'

From then on I read the questions ahead of time and researched the answers. And I vowed that if I didn't know the answer to a question I would be honest about it. Despite the rocky start I ended up having excellent relationships with the students' families. I'm sure they didn't send their daughters to a private all-girls school only to have a young cricket tragic with peroxide-blond hair teach them, but I think they realised that what I was doing was somehow good for their girls.

I never told any of the parents that my approach – being straightforward, engaging with their daughters on their own terms, and incorporating strategies to reduce stress and anxiety – was informed by my keenly felt imperative to not see them suffer the way my parents had.

I developed the most wonderful relationships with my Year 5 girls, partly because I created something of a sporting-club culture in the classroom. For instance, I gave every single girl a nickname and I still remember them to this day: Lippy, Junior, MacDaddy, Fuzz, Sir Charles and all the rest. I also strongly believed that students should absolutely love coming to school, as high levels of positive emotional engagement are the key to any learning environment.

On the first day of my second year teaching Year 5, I gathered my class of newcomers together ten minutes before the last bell. 'There's something you should know about this school,' I told them. 'One of the water bubblers has Coke in it. You twist the tap and Coke comes out. We're one of only a few schools in Australia that has one. OK, you've got five minutes to find it.'

They took off in search of the fabled Coca-Cola bubbler among the dozens of bubblers throughout the school grounds. I watched from the classroom as they tore back and forth through the playground, feverishly searching for soft drink. Before long I was in hysterics. I quickly gathered myself when one of the girls burst back into the room and begged me, 'Which one is it, sir? I'm not allowed to have Coke at home. Please, *pleeeease* tell me!'

'Sorry,' I deadpanned. 'You're going to have to find it.'

When the final bell rang a few minutes later they all came back, covered in water and sweat, to collect their bags.

'Did you find it?' I asked.

'*Nooo!*' they chorused.

'Oh, it must have been turned off. Sorry, girls, tomorrow we'll find it.'

At 2.55 pm the following day, I let them go for it again. There was a stampede for the door but five minutes later they returned looking more miffed than disappointed.

'Which one is it?' MacDaddy demanded.

I decided it was time to let up. 'I was only joking,' I laughed. 'As if there would be Coke coming out of the water bubblers. That's a lesson in gullibility, girls. If something sounds too good to be true, it usually is.'

Junior and Sir Charles fixed me with that screwed-up face of disgust only tweenage girls can conjure and said, 'We'll get you back.'

'No, you won't,' I said, trying to sound like a serious authority figure. 'Not a chance!'

Five months later we received a new whiz-bang smartboard to be mounted on our classroom wall. It had arrived in some huge cardboard boxes, and after I unpacked the thing I kicked the empty boxes into a corner behind my desk.

One day the kids went out for lunch as usual, and when they returned I had them sit down and do some silent reading. That's when I noticed we were two students short. 'Where are Junior and Sir Charles?' I said.

'I don't know,' one of the other girls replied. 'They were

sort of standing around the front gate at lunchtime but they're gone. I think they left.'

'What do you mean they left?' I said, trying not to sound panicked.

'I don't know,' the girl said. 'We saw them there and now they're gone!'

'WHAT?' I screeched. 'Oh my God!'

I sprinted out of the classroom and did several laps around the school. I didn't even bother to get someone to look after my class because I didn't want to admit I'd lost two kids. When I couldn't find them anywhere I started to properly freak out. I ran into classrooms asking, 'Has anyone seen Junior or Sir Charles?' only to be met with quizzical looks and shaking heads.

It was the stuff of nightmares. I had lost two ten-year-old girls who had last been seen near the gate that led straight onto a main road. Horror scenarios flashed through my mind. I staggered back into my classroom and slumped into my chair, close to tears.

'Are you alright, sir?' someone asked.

'Yeah, it's fine,' I replied in a quavering voice. 'I've just got to call the principal.'

As soon as I picked up the phone there was a clamorous noise in the corner of the room as Junior and Sir Charles burst out of the empty cardboard boxes and scared the living daylights out of me. I nearly fainted as 30 girls shrieked with laughter.

'We told you we'd get you back,' Junior said.

As much as I wanted to be angry at them, the episode reassured me that I was on the right track with my approach; the girls were willing to take risks and work together to deliver on a promise, even if it was at my expense.

It was obvious a lot of the girls came from structured, regimented homes. Their parents wanted the very best for them academically and were generally strict on appearance, grooming, study and homework. I took study seriously too, but I also threw in some curve balls now and then when it came to homework.

Once a week we did what became known as YouTube Tuesday. I'd ferret around on the internet and look for the weirdest, most obscure YouTube video I could find and play it for the kids on a Monday afternoon. The first time I did it, their faces contorted with confusion and they asked, 'What the hell is this?'

'This is your homework tonight,' I explained.

The clip was of a strange man dressed in a high-collared, old-fashioned English outfit, doing something called 'The

Little Lad Dance'. As he pranced about like a twit, he sang the 'Berries and Cream' song:

Berries and cream, berries and cream,
I'm a little lad who likes berries and cream.

It was weird but terrific. Google it.

'I want you all to go home and learn that dance tonight, girls,' I said, 'because tomorrow we're all going to be doing it together.'

I made them put it in their homework diaries because I wanted their parents to know that this year was going to be different. The girls were being pushed beyond their comfort zone of study, blazers and perfectly done hair. 'There's no maths and no literacy tonight,' I continued. 'Homework is to learn the Berries and Cream dance, memorise all the moves, and then tomorrow, when you least expect it, I'm going to yell out "Berries and Cream!" and you'll bust out the dance.'

I remember the girls giggling with anticipation the next morning as they made their way into the classroom, and I overheard whispered conversations about the moves they found most difficult. When class began, I pretended I'd forgotten about their homework; in fact, I acted a bit grumpy to throw them off guard.

One of the girls put her hand up. 'Mr V, have you forgotten something?'

'I haven't forgotten that it's time for maths!' I said enthusiastically.

Three hours later, when I sensed that the girls had given up hope, I announced in my most serious tone, 'Girls, please put down your pens. I have an announcement: "Berries and Cream!"'

The girls threw themselves into the activity with a level of dedication I hadn't seen coming. Just as they were finishing the dance, I yelled out the words again, and we repeated the cycle. We did the dance about six times in a row. I'd never seen them laugh so hard, and I'd never laughed so hard either.

Research tells us that there are three things that instantly promote a positive shift in our emotional state: music, exercise and laughter.[1] I've made a concerted effort to integrate these gems in my day-to-day life, and the Berries and Cream dance was the ultimate combination of all three. It was a group activity that made the girls feel like they were part of something special, leading to a warmer and more inclusive classroom environment. When you're happy to make a fool of yourself in front of your peers, making yourself vulnerable, it's particularly difficult to be judgemental of others.

I also used a variety of odd techniques to get the best out of the girls academically. If they worked hard and in silence for 40 minutes I would occasionally reward them with a silent dance party.

'I want you all to focus on your maths for the next forty minutes, without making a sound, and if you can do that I'll let you dance for three minutes to whatever song you want to play in your head,' I promised.

'What if the principal sees us?' someone asked.

'If the principal sees us, believe me, I'll get in trouble – not you guys!' I said. 'Just work hard now and you can have a silent dance party.'

After 40 minutes of the girls converting improper fractions into mixed numbers, I said, 'Pens down. It's on!'

I pressed play on the boom box but no noise came out. 'Oh, that's right,' I said. 'It's a silent dance party. There is no song and you can't make any noise whatsoever – you've just gotta dance. Go!'

For the next three minutes the classroom became a zoo as 30 girls twisted, bopped and twirled in complete silence. It was something to behold. Anyone passing by or looking through the window would not have known what to make of it. Fortunately no one ever found out – certainly not the principal. At least I hope not.

I was determined to model behaviours that I felt were key to living a happier life, in particular learning to embrace our imperfections. When it came time to teach the girls about symmetry, I just so happened to have a pimple erupt right in the middle of my forehead. I had the girls measure the distance from my ears to the pimple. They calculated it was exactly the same distance from each ear to the pimple, so I drew a thick line down the centre of my face with a marker. 'That,' I said, pointing at my face, 'is symmetry.' We took a photo of my face, printed it out, and stuck the photo on our noticeboard, where it stayed for months.

Back in 2006, I wasn't aware that the Western world was about to be taken over by a perfectionist epidemic. Social media has deepened our impression that everyone else's life is perfect, because we only see the 'greatest hits' on Facebook and Instagram, and this increases our struggle when things in our own life aren't going the way we'd hoped they would. I'm sure most of my students know now what symmetry is, but what I truly hope they remember from the lesson is that we're all imperfect, and the more we share our imperfections and the more vulnerable we make ourselves to others, the more we open ourselves up to joy through meaningful connection.

I was trying to figure out an approach to pastoral teaching

and student wellbeing on the fly. I wasn't reading enough about it, though, so I asked my fellow teachers what they were doing around wellbeing. The answer was pretty much nothing. I was too young and too inexperienced to take it up at curricular level with the principal, so I just went about doing my own thing.

Because of what my family had been through with Georgia, I took a huge interest in kids who were struggling. After a while, older girls would seek me out in the playground and chat about friendship issues or family problems they wanted to share. I found myself an unofficial counsellor to them.

I never gave the students advice; I'd just sit and listen, which is often what people need the most – validation for their feelings of anxiety, sadness, anger, loneliness. But I was always fascinated by these girls, and knew that somehow I'd be able to help them somewhere along the line. I grew to be envious of the school counsellor. 'What a great job,' I'd think to myself. 'Imagine helping people with their problems rather than trying to teach them long division. That's what calculators are for.'

Importantly, I started to feel that I was *meant* to be working in some kind of counselling role; that maybe this could be a new kind of purpose in life. I was definitely on the right path. My thinking was that the harder I worked on teaching with an emphasis on pastoral care, the less chance there would be of my students suffering the way Georgia had.

I couldn't wait for the next school year to start.

CHAPTER 4
DISCOVERING HAPPINESS

I really didn't want to go to India.

I was happy in Melbourne. I had a fulfilling job with a renewed sense of purpose and a hometown brimming with opportunities to do the things I loved. Cricket remained a source of joy, and I was lucky enough to be sharing a house close to the MCG. If I was hungry I could walk to my favourite cafes. If I fancied a beer I could pull up a stool in my local pub and if I was craving social or psychological nourishment I was blessed with amazing friends and family. Why would I want to suddenly go to India?

Her name was Anjali.

We'd met at university – she was also studying education – and I had fallen hopelessly in love. Anjali was half-Indian and half-Australian, and she was absolutely stunning both inside and out. The first time I saw her, in the computer lab at uni, my jaw was on the floor. When she happened to turn up to my next class, in a rare moment of courage I went and sat next to her then introduced myself in a nervous, quavering, high-pitched voice. Convincing her that we should be more than just friends was a lengthy process – perhaps one of my greatest trials of resilience.

I was so enamoured of Anjali that I tended to do whatever she wanted. She wasn't pushy or controlling in any way; it's just that I felt compelled to do anything to make her happy. If she wanted sushi for lunch, we ate raw fish; if she wanted to go for a walk in the rain, I gladly got wet. I treated her every wish as my command, and in 2008 Anjali wished to go and live in India for half a year.

I had just coached my beloved MUCC to a club championship, so things were looking good for me again in the cricketing world, this time as a coach. But as much as I wanted to stay home and focus on my cricket and my work at Fintona, I soon found myself stepping off a plane and into the madness that is Mumbai. My initial emotional response to India was abject fear. As far as I could see, the place was completely out of control. Ten million cars with horns blaring choked the roads alongside 20 million people on foot, not to mention cows and other animals that randomly appeared amid the traffic.

Legions of beggars – the destitute and the disabled – reached out at every turn, while basic sanitation, let alone a functioning sewerage system, seemed not to exist. People would stare at us. I was beyond anxious, and I just wanted to go home. The images of families sleeping by the side of the road, with cars whizzing past them, is something I will never get out of my head.

It took weeks for me to even begin to relax, go with the flow and start to appreciate the subcontinent's limitless majestic charms. We visited some of Anjali's distant relatives, we travelled the west coast on a shoestring budget, and I even started to look for opportunities for a game of cricket. God knows millions of kids were constantly playing it out on the street.

One afternoon, I found myself wandering the busy streets of Mumbai when I came across a boy who was playing a different kind of game. He was dressed only in a pair of tattered shorts and was alone, but he seemed to be having the time of his life. He'd tied a piece of string to a plastic bag and was darting back and forth in the street as if he was running on an empty beach flying a beautiful kite.

'Would you like to have a go?' he asked in broken English when he saw me taking an interest in what he was doing. So I gave his makeshift kite a quick twirl, hoping to give a good impression of someone having a wonderful time. Always a teacher, I asked him where he went to school.

'Oh, would you like to see the school?' he replied.

'Yes, I'd love to,' I said.

The boy led me to a dilapidated timber building that was barely clinging to the banks of the polluted river that ran through the city. Although it looked as though it would eventually slide off its foundations and sink into the murky grey water, 130 children aged around five to 16 were crammed inside and sat on the floor facing a blackboard. There was only one teacher on duty and it looked like she'd ruled the board into five columns. She was in the process of teaching five lessons at once, from kindergarten right through to around Year 10.

In an Australian school it would be fair to expect this approach to result in some noisy disruption at best, total chaos at worst. But there wasn't a word in this teacher's classroom; she had the children's complete attention. You could have heard a pin drop. 'This woman,' I thought to myself, 'has the most extraordinary classroom management skills I have ever seen.'

I didn't want to disturb the class so I quietly left this superhero teacher to her work. Outside I asked the boy in the ripped shorts why he wasn't in school that day.

'Oh, I don't go to school,' he said.

'Really? Why not?'

'I'm not lucky,' he replied. 'Only the lucky people get to go to school.' It was a pretty heartbreaking thing to hear a child say.

He scurried off with his string and plastic bag, and I never saw him again.

Anjali had been talking about doing some teaching in India, and the encounter with the boy led to another conversation on the subject. I'd initially resisted the idea of working while on holiday, but after a couple of months I started to think it might not be such a bad idea. There were plenty of excellent private schools in India, so I figured we could get paid quite well to help fund our travels. It also occurred to me that working in a top school would likely lead to some cricket coaching.

'No, I think we should volunteer instead,' Anjali countered.

'Really?'

'Yes. We should volunteer at a school for underprivileged children. Why would we go and work in a private school, where there are plenty of great teachers, when we could go and volunteer at a school that desperately needs extra staff?'

Anjali possessed a beautiful, compassionate outlook on the world – something I clearly hadn't quite yet developed. As ever, her wish was my command. Anjali made some inquiries, which led to arrangements for us to travel to a remote village in the folds of the Himalayas in the far north of India.

Nothing could have prepared me for the beauty of the place. The village was located in the Ladakh region of Jammu state, close to Indian-controlled Kashmir. It's almost 2400 kilometres from Mumbai, but as far as I could see it was a million miles from the rest of planet Earth.

If you google classic images of India you'll invariably see a thousand photos of the Taj Mahal, of Hindu women in bright saris with dots painted on their foreheads, or wizened old men in turbans. The part of India we were now standing in was unlike anything I had ever seen, even in photos.

The village sat on the edge of a high-altitude desert plain ringed by precarious snow-capped peaks that reached breathtakingly into a vivid blue sky. The villagers appeared more Tibetan than Indian, and they struck me as the nicest, most gracious people I had ever met. Every person I encountered would clasp their hands in front of their face, bow towards me and repeatedly give their traditional greeting in the Ladhaki language: 'Jullay, jullay'.

Anjali had organised for us to teach the local children English and instruct the teachers how to educate people in English so that the work would continue after we'd left. The school principal was good enough to put us up in his home, a modest mud hut. Like everybody else in the village we slept on the floor. The principal had a TV he was extremely proud of, even though it remained turned off because electricity was only available for a handsome fee.

Despite the dazzling scenery and the innate friendliness of the locals, I still felt very insecure and reckoned I'd only be able to spend a couple of days, tops, in the village. It might have been beautiful but most buildings had no power, no running water and no sewerage system. It was well outside my comfort zone, and that was before I was struck down by a severe bout of altitude sickness.

After two days spent either sleeping or throwing up at the principal's house, I overcame the illness and arrived at the school weakened but ready to teach.

I had no idea I was the one who would do the most learning.

The L-shaped mud-brick school rose unremarkably out of the hard, dry Himalayan desert plain. It was a fairly basic institution; most classrooms had only one table and one chair for the teachers, while the students sat on the dirt floor. The view through the windows, however, was like that of no other school on the planet: across the other side of the shimmering desert a jagged brown-grey mountain range ruptured the Earth's surface in the most dramatic fashion.

There were around 150 children enrolled at the school, ranging from four to 16 years of age. As with the classroom full of students I'd observed in Mumbai a few weeks before, the children were well behaved, quiet and attentive. But there was something else notable about the kids in the village: each and every one of them seemed to be in great spirits every day. They radiated happiness.

Early in our stay the principal assigned four of the Year 3 boys to show me around the school grounds. The first stop — the thing they were most eager to show me — was the play equipment. Never before had I beheld such a depressing sight in a school playground.

The 'equipment' comprised a swing set and a seesaw that would have looked at home in post-meltdown Chernobyl. The swings were either missing or broken; instead, rusted metal chains of varying length dangled forlornly in the thin mountain air.

The seesaw was more of an eyesore than anything else; it was rusted fast and didn't work either. Like the dilapidated swing set, the seesaw was painted in faded bands of yellow and red which brought to mind the vibrant markings on venomous creatures in nature – a clear warning to stay away.

My little tour guides stood in front of this haphazard tangle of useless metal and jerked their thumbs at it. 'Hey sir,' they said, 'look at this.'

At first I thought they were pointing out how underwhelming it was, as in, 'Hey sir, have you ever seen anything more miserable? Isn't this sad? In our entire school all we have is broken swings and a seesaw that doesn't work.'

It took me a moment, however, to realise they were in fact saying, 'Hey sir, how cool is *this* set-up?' They were excited and proud to show me their amazing play equipment. The kids absolutely loved it. They didn't need it to work the way it had been designed to; they invented different games to play on it, including swinging on the rusty chains or just hanging off them for as long as they could.

One of the boys was suspended from a chain when I walked by the next morning. 'Hey sir,' he called out, 'in your country, do children in schools get the same play equipment that we have?'

I thought about how best to answer him. My initial instinct was to be expansive and say, 'Mate, you should see what we have. We have basketball courts, synthetic ovals, all kinds of sporting equipment, the classrooms have carpet and chairs for the kids, heaters and air-conditioners and dozens of taps with water in them. We have electricity with lights you can turn on and off, laptop computers and these amazing things called "smartboards". And that's just at school.'

But as he contentedly dangled from the chain with a huge smile on his face, I simply replied, 'Yes. Kids in Australia do have the same play equipment as you guys.'

'That makes me happy,' the boy said, before jumping to the ground and running inside for class.

I was besotted with all of the children at the school, but one boy completely stole my heart. His name was Stanzin, he was nine years old and he remains the kindest person I have ever met.

The first time I walked into Stanzin's classroom I didn't notice how low the doorframe was and I smacked my forehead upon entry. I reeled about, clutching my head like I was

Kramer in an episode of *Seinfeld*. I had never seen a group of kids laugh so much in my entire life.

When I walked back into the classroom the following day, little Stanzin was standing near the doorway, looking up towards the ceiling with a big smile on his face.

'Good morning, Stanzin,' I said. 'What are you smiling at?'

He pointed up at the top of the doorframe. He had found a length of cloth and filled it with sand and leaves, then tied it on the spot where I'd nearly knocked myself out the day before.

'Did you make that for me?' I asked him.

'Yes,' said Stanzin. 'Yesterday was bad.'

'Thank you, Stanzin,' I said. 'That's kind of you.'

He smiled again and beckoned me to look down the hallway.

'What is it?' I asked.

'Every door!' Stanzin replied, tapping his fingers to his forehead as if to relive the previous day's tragicomic head-whacking. Indeed Stanzin had rigged each doorway he deemed a danger to me with some kind of DIY padding.

I was beyond touched and found myself genuinely speechless at this little boy's act of kindness. I soon realised I wasn't the only person Stanzin showed a genuine concern for. If he ever noticed one of his classmates was by themselves at lunchtime, Stanzin would stop whatever he was doing and go straight over to them. 'Are you alright?' he would ask. 'Do you want to come and play with us?'

Whenever someone was sick, he would drop by their home after school to check that they were doing OK. No matter what was going on in his life, Stanzin would put it to one side in order to help someone else. Even when he was playing his favourite game, cricket.

One lunchtime Stanzin was batting, scoring well and clearly having a blast. He was about to face another delivery (of a ball made out of rubber bands wrapped together) and was scanning the field for where to place his next shot when he noticed a Year 1 girl sitting by herself. Stanzin promptly dropped the bat and played with the little girl until lunchtime ended.

'This kid,' I said to Anjali later, 'has got to be the most caring, selfless and truly happy person I have ever met.' Within a few days I had gone from thinking I couldn't possibly last in the village to being barely able to wait to get to school each day so I could spend time with the children, especially my little mate Stanzin.

Sadly, Anjali's grandma died a couple of weeks into the trip. Anjali was devastated, and planned to return to

Melbourne as soon as she could. As she was making arrangements, I found myself wandering the streets of the village one night, faced with the prospect of returning to Australia. As I made my way back to the mud-brick home we were staying in, I saw something that changed my life forever.

It was my little mate Stanzin in his school uniform, getting ready to go to sleep. I went over to him and said hello. He was sleeping on the ground in basic conditions, like many other people in the village. I shouldn't have been shocked, but the image really hit me. He had a huge smile on his face. I smiled back at him as I said goodbye and turned around to head home, all the while fighting an overwhelming urge to cry.

I didn't sleep a wink that night. I thought of all the people I knew back home in Australia, and the students I'd taught over the years who'd struggled with depression, anxiety and other mental illnesses. Why were we in the developed world so broken? Why were we in Australia, such a beautiful and privileged country, so anxious and depressed? There were so many questions bouncing around in my mind.

It wasn't just Stanzin who seemed to have found the secret to happiness; virtually everyone I had got to know in this remote village was the same. I'm not suggesting that people in developing nations don't struggle with mental ill health;

but I did know that there was something very special about the attitude of the villagers based on my experience there.

When I returned to our home that night, I broached the sensitive topic of my not returning home with Anjali for the funeral. I was in love with the place and knew I couldn't leave. I had to stay as long as it took to figure out the answer to the burning question: what did Stanzin do every day to make him so happy? Being the ever-compassionate and dedicated teacher that she is, Anjali said she would return from Melbourne as soon as she'd given her grandmother a proper farewell.

Stanzin would turn up to class each day with a notebook and a pencil, and so did I – in order to take notes on him. I kept a very close eye on what he did each day and studied his patterns of behaviour. I already knew he was an extremely kind person but I wanted to unravel what it was that made him that way.

The kids used to slip their shoes off before going into class and put them back on when it was time to go outside. One lunchtime, as they were running out to play, I walked over to Stanzin as he was lacing up his shoes.

'Sir, look. Look!' he said, pointing at his feet. 'Sir, dis!'

In Ladakh, people find it almost impossible to make the 'th' sound with their tongue pressed behind their teeth, so I knew Stanzin was saying 'this'. The message was, 'Sir, look at this! Look at my shoes. Isn't it awesome that I'm lucky enough to have shoes on my feet?'

He was well aware that not all of his friends had a pair of shoes. By the look of them, Stanzin had owned his cherished shoes for a couple of years because, as his feet grew bigger, he'd cut the ends off the uppers to allow his toes to protrude from the end.

It wasn't just shoes the kids struggled to afford. Most didn't have anything to bring to school for lunch, so each day we fed them plain rice. The way Stanzin and his friends reacted when presented with a bowl of rice, you'd have thought they were eating chocolate cake.

'Sir, dis! Dis!' Stanzin would say, jabbing his index finger at the bowl between mouthfuls. In other words, 'Sir, how good is it that we get lunch at school? Can you believe how good this is?' Then they'd all charge outside to play on the school's celebrated red-and-yellow play equipment like it was the most exciting ride at Luna Park.

Above all else, however, Stanzin seemed to value his friends. I'd watch the students play at lunchtime and whenever he saw me he'd stop whatever he was doing and individually point out his playmates. 'Sir, dis person and dis person and dis person and dis person . . .'

He wanted to acknowledge how lucky he felt to have friends. Sometimes the level of love and happiness in that dusty schoolyard almost made me cry. It was the most beautiful community I had ever had the privilege to visit.

Another thing I noticed the villagers did that we don't really do back in Australia was meditation. I'm not talking about just now and then; as devout Buddhists, they meditated every single day. Between 8.30 and 9 am – before classes started – the students would assemble in the yard, where they would sit in silence and focus on being in the present moment. 'So, they're praying are they?' I'd asked the English teacher when I'd first arrived in the village.

'No,' he said. 'They're doing meditation.'

I scoffed inwardly and thought, 'What a ridiculous waste of time. Surely the kids would rather be doing something more enjoyable than sitting still at the start of every day.' But then it was pointed out to me that meditation at the school was 100 per cent optional. The kids didn't have to attend if they didn't want to, but every child turned up early because they didn't want to miss out. There had to be something in that.

Eventually I decided to join in. I wasn't exactly sitting among them cross-legged, but I did remain to the side, still and silent, paying attention to these incredible sessions. Once I got the hang of tuning out the noise of thoughts running through my mind, the sessions began to have a profound impact on me.

Before I started meditating I'd often worried about the things I was missing back home: how was Georgia? How were my beloved Hawthorn Football Club going? How was pre-season cricket training going without me around? After two weeks of the practice, I felt a marked improvement in my mood and mental clarity. I understood why no one skipped meditation – I was totally present.

Twelve years after Georgia had first been diagnosed with a mental illness, I felt as though I was finding out the answer to the question I'd been asking myself ever since: what makes us happy? The people of the village definitely weren't impervious to trauma, sadness, hardship and loss, but they dealt with the vicissitudes of life differently to the way I'd been used to. After an incredible three months living in the village, I felt I understood why they were such a happy community. Ultimately, there were three principles they practised every day that were key to their resilient worldview and happy disposition:

GRATITUDE

Ever since this trip, I have described gratitude as the ability to pay attention to what you have, instead of worrying about what you don't have. Too many of us in Australia live by a model of happiness known as the 'if and then' model: *If* I buy this car, *then* I will feel happy. *If* I get this promotion, *then* I will feel happy. *If* we buy and live in a house like this, *then* we will feel happy. But the 'if and then' approach doesn't work; months after we buy a new car, we'll see a better car and think that's our key to happiness. We have so much available to us in Australia, but we miss what we have all the time because we're too focused on what we don't have.

I was lying awake in the village one night when it occurred to me I had witnessed this kind of gratitude before. It was in the tumbledown school next to the polluted river in Mumbai, where the class of 130 students somehow remained totally focused on learning.

At the time I put their concentration down to the teacher's excellent classroom management skills. While she was no doubt a great educator, what I most likely witnessed that day was gratitude; those children knew they were lucky to be at school and that not everyone got to go to school, so they weren't going to miss a second of it.

Young Stanzin went a step further and actively practised gratitude in the moment. If he was feeling lucky to have a few friends to play cricket with, he took the time to think about it and even point it out. 'Dis person and dis person,' or 'Dis pair of shoes, dis bowl of rice.' He focused on the good things he had, not what he didn't have.

The other students all practised gratitude in their own way, too, whether it was being thankful for the opportunity to have a daily meditation class or proud that their school boasted a remarkable swing set and seesaw.

EMPATHY

Empathy is the ability to psychologically feel what another person is feeling. The more empathetic we are, the more likely we are to act in a kind way, and the neuroscience behind kindness is incredible. When you do something kind for someone else, your brain releases oxytocin, which is known as the 'love hormone'.[1] Why? Because oxytocin allows us to feel joy, happiness and love. And we don't even need to perform grand acts of kindness; simpler acts like holding the door open for someone, letting someone in front of you in traffic or giving someone a genuine compliment can do the trick.

I learned more about empathy from Stanzin than from any person before or since. Stanzin felt my pain when I cracked my head on the doorframe – so much so that he wanted to prevent me from ever feeling that way again. It was the same reason he was endlessly kind towards everyone in his life. He felt compelled to make them feel safe, included, special and happy. Importantly, I could see that this approach to life also made Stanzin feel happy. A win-win.

The other students displayed a well-developed sense of empathy, too. I thought back to the little boy who wanted to know whether kids in Australia had the same play equipment as he did at his school. When I said they did, his response was telling: 'That,' he said, 'makes me happy.' The knowledge that some abstract children in a far-off land were blessed with the same things he had made *him* feel happy.

MINDFULNESS

The villagers were calm, measured and patient. When I first arrived in their midst I was the opposite; stressed and somewhat anxious to leave. After three months living among them, however, I realised that while they faced daily hardships, pressures and concerns – in fact, their hardships were more immediate and acute than most of ours in the West – they managed their responses differently. The key to this, I discovered, was mindfulness – taking time to focus solely on the present moment.

After I started meditating with the children and teachers each day, I found I spent less time worrying about what might happen in the future or things that had happened in the past. I instead focused more and more on the life I was living in that given moment. When I spoke to someone, I became totally focused on the conversation. When I taught the children, there was nothing else crowding my thoughts. I realised that practising mindfulness – meditating – was a way of taking greater control of your mind and, therefore, your life.

So much for the guy who didn't want to go to India. The trip was a watershed in my life. There is pre-India Hugh and post-India Hugh. As much as I had loved my time on the subcontinent, though, I was excited to return to Australia.

I was as keen as ever to throw myself into my cricket and I was dying to catch up with my friends and family. Most of all, I was desperate to get back into the classroom so I could integrate all of these lessons into my own teaching.

CHAPTER 5

CHIEF MOTIVATIONAL OFFICER

'Well, excuse my language – but that's fucked!'

I had just told a student in my new class that I barracked for the Hawthorn Football Club. He didn't like it one bit.

I'd been back from India for ten months and was going through a terrible period in my personal life. I was devastated when Anjali and I broke up, and my amazing Granny June had just passed away.

Still, I'd landed a job at SEDA College, a specialised campus for Years 11 and 12. There I taught a class of young people who struggled to learn in a traditional setting. I threw myself into work and hoped I'd be able to distract myself from sinking into a dark place.

One of the students was an 18-year-old named Nick Burke who went by the nickname 'Beefy'. He caught my attention on the first day by asking all kinds of unusual questions. When the final bell rang and all the other students had left, Beefy decided to hang around and talk footy with me.

That afternoon I discovered Beefy was the most passionate Collingwood supporter to ever walk upon the Earth, and that if he feels you are challenging the club in any way he flicks the emotional switch. Beefy possessed an encyclopaedic knowledge of Collingwood, its players and its history, and he worshipped the club great and current coach Nathan Buckley as if he were a deity.

Just when I thought Beefy was never going to stop banging on about the Magpies and Nathan Buckley, he fell silent for a moment and sort of sized me up in the empty classroom.

'So, who do you support?' He thrust his hands on his hips and puffed his chest out, waiting for my reply.

'The Hawks, mate,' I replied with a smile. That's when he voiced his utter disgust towards me, in language that left much to be desired.

'Whoa-whoa-whoa!' I said, a bit startled by his use of the

F-word. 'Mate, we're in school. I'm your teacher. You can't say things like that!'

'I did say "excuse my language",' Beefy said, doubling down. 'How can you be my "teacher" –' he threw his hands either side of his head to indicate inverted commas – 'if you barrack for the Hawks?' To my amusement, he also made inverted commas around 'Hawks'.

I could already tell that this kid was an absolute legend. He had that certain something, and it was all I could do to stop myself laughing. For a moment I forgot I was struggling with the loss of my granny and my relationship. 'This kid,' I thought, 'is a beauty. I absolutely love him!'

Nobody had bothered to tell me that Beefy had cerebral palsy and hydrocephalus (too much fluid on his brain), or that he'd suffered a stroke on the day he was born. When I found out, it put things into a bit of perspective. But only a bit; Beefy might have had limitations to his range of physical movement and his learning capacities, but when it came to passion, humour, warmth, kindness and a zest for life, he was limitless. As a teacher you're not supposed to have favourites but, well, I had Beefy.

Over the next 12 months, Beefy and I teased each other nonstop in class. He didn't know it but he also helped me overcome my emotional pain.

Beefy struggled academically so I had to think laterally to get him through the final year of his education. For the major English assessment, for example, the class had to write a thousand words on something they felt passionate about.

'What are you thinking, Beefy?' I asked him.

'Nathan Buckley,' came the steely reply.

While the subject of his essay on passion was a no-brainer, Beefy was faced with a challenge. In his own words, his handwriting was 'shockin', mate', and using a laptop was difficult for him – though he seemed to manage just fine when it came to looking up YouTube videos of Nathan Buckley – so I suggested he deliver his assignment as a speech instead.

When the day came, Beefy stood up in class and reeled off one of the most emotional addresses I had ever heard from someone so young. Halfway through the speech he had to take a moment to recompose himself because he'd started to cry – he loved Nathan Buckley and Collingwood that much. There was more passion in Beefy's words that day than in any of the written essays that were handed in. He passed with flying colours.

I wasn't sure what path Beefy was going to take after high school, but for the time being he had a part-time job as a cleaner at his local McDonald's. He took it very seriously and loved the fact he was pulling in cash to spend on following his beloved Magpies around the country.

One day Beefy didn't show up to school. It was completely out of character and I was a little worried, so I phoned him.

'Where are you, mate?'

'I got fired from my job,' he said. 'I'm a bit flat.'

Because of his limited movement, Beefy wasn't quite able to do the cleaning job properly. It was a busy McDonald's outlet and he was just too slow to keep up with the pace, so they had to let him go. The poor kid was shattered.

'But what about school, Beefy?' I said. 'We haven't sacked you. We need you here!'

'Nah, I'm not going to school,' he said. 'I don't feel like it.'

I had to come up with something fast so I blurted out, 'Beefy, don't feel too bad about McDonald's, mate, because I've actually got a job for you.'

'Oh yeah?' he said, suddenly sounding more like himself. 'What is it?'

The conversation had unfolded quickly and I hadn't given any thought to what job I might be able to find for him. I had to buy myself some time. 'Listen, mate,' I said, 'if you come to school I'll tell you what the job is, OK?'

Beefy turned up about half an hour later.

'So what's this job?' he asked.

'Well, we need a water boy,' I replied.

'Who's we? For what?'

'For my cricket club! We need a water boy.'

'Are you serious?'

'Yeah. Do you want to do it?'

'Fucking oath!'

'Beefy, stop swearing. We're at school,' I said. But then I leaned in close and lowered my voice so only he could hear: 'We'd fucking love to have you, you bloody legend. Do you know how to be a water boy?'

'Yeah,' he said confidently. 'Of course I do.'

'We'll see you at Round One then,' I said. 'Round One will be in two months' time.'

'Righto. I'll be there.' He fixed me with a deadly serious look that just screamed commitment.

During the off-season, our cricket club trained at a hockey pitch (part of the club's facilities) adjacent to our home ground. Two weeks after I offered Beefy the water boy position, he arrived at training unannounced. God knows how he found out when and where we trained, but there he was. As coach I was halfway through addressing the players when he came over.

'G'day, Beefman! What are you doing here?' I said.

'I've come to training,' he replied with a shrug. 'I've gotta practise.'

The rest of the guys looked at me as if to say, 'Who's this bloke?' so I introduced him. 'Boys, I'd like you to meet Beefy. Beefy, meet the boys. OK, everybody, so Beefy is our water boy. Trust me, you're gonna love him.'

It was pretty obvious that Beefy wasn't your average water boy. For one thing, his cerebral palsy caused him to shuffle rather than walk, let alone dash about the place. A little later on, one or two of the guys pulled me aside and said, 'What do we need a water boy for?'

'I don't know,' I replied. 'We just need one. He's our water boy.'

'Really?'

'Yep. We need him. Trust me.'

He may not have been the fastest water boy in Victorian grade cricket, but by God he was the most committed. From that night onwards Beefy was the first one to get to training, even though it took him an hour and a half on public transport. Without fail, he'd be at the oval waiting for us with his rack of plastic water bottles. Sometimes they were full, sometimes they weren't.

We were going through some drills a few weeks later

when Beefy came over and started handing empty water bottles to the players.

'Beefy,' someone piped up, 'there's no water in this.'

'Yeah, I know,' he said with a little grin as he handed out more of them. 'I couldn't be fucked filling them up today.'

'So what am I meant to do with an empty water bottle?' the player inquired.

'Fuck, I dunno!' Beefy shot back with a shrug. 'You'll work it out. You're smart – you're university students, aren't you?'

It brought the house down. The boys were on the ground, laughing at Beefy's ridiculous charm. That's when everybody realised that yes, our club most definitely did need a water boy – but only if it was Beefy.

Beefy quickly became a cult figure at the Melbourne University Cricket Club. If he wasn't handing out water bottles (or air bottles), he was talking animatedly about his beloved Collingwood Magpies. He loved his cricket too and would always dissect our games, albeit via a stream of old-school AFL clichés.

Before long Beefy was chiming in on the coaches' analysis of the games, and I sometimes had to ask him to back off a little. His comments were very honest, and any advice for the coaches was delivered as if he was preparing the Magpies to play a grand final in front of 100,000 people: 'Boys, you've got to want it, and if you don't want it it's not going to turn up on a silver fucking platter for you, is it? You've got to want it, so go out there and fucking get it!'

Sometimes it was just what we needed to hear, but other times – particularly after a hard defeat – well, not so much. On those occasions I'd have to say, 'Beefy, not today, mate.'

After a few years, when Beefy was a bona fide club identity and I was still coaching, we had a bad weekend when we lost in all four grades. At training the following week, Beefy sidled up to me with his water bottles.

'The boys are flat tonight,' he said.

'What was that?' I replied. I was pretty down and I didn't really feel like analysis from the Beefton.

'I said the boys are flat tonight,' he repeated.

'I know, Beefy. We had a very bad weekend, so . . . yeah.'

'Not good enough,' he said evenly.

'What?!' I shot back, a little annoyed.

'Not good enough,' he said again, then turned to face me directly. Beefy pointed at me in his particular way, using his open right hand. 'I'd give anything to go and play cricket like these boys, Hugh, but I can't,' he said. 'Take a look at 'em – they're sulking because they lost? Not good enough!'

Beefy might as well have squirted a water bottle in my face. Suddenly I was five-year-old Hugh again, the one who'd just had a tantrum and thrown his bat against the fence in the backyard in Balwyn. That day, Dad had taught me that it matters how you carry yourself in defeat, and now Beefy had just reminded me. 'Mate, that's brilliant,' I said. 'Thank you. I needed it.'

Beefy returned his gaze to the players who were still gingerly going through the motions out on the oval. 'Bring 'em in,' he said.

'What are you talking about?'

'Just bring 'em all in, mate,' he said, with a beckoning wave of his hand. 'They need to hear it from me.'

He was absolutely right, so I called all the players together. Over the next few minutes Beefy proceeded to give us the most almighty spray we have ever copped.

'You know what, boys?' he said. 'Cricket is a bit like running, right? It's like athletics. It's like a race. So, "Oh yeah, we've had a good season." Oh yeah, we haven't got out of first gear yet if you ask me!

'It's like we've reached the final lap and that bell's ringing, boys, the bell's ringing, and I tell you what – time to get out of first gear and fucking burn the shit out of them!'

We were immediately pumped, and right behind Beefy. We let out a huge cheer and the boys were about to walk off when Beefy yelled, 'Stop – get back here!'

When he had everyone's attention again he looked around the group one final time and roared, 'No complacency!'

They boys went nuts, cheering, chanting, 'No complacency!', high-fiving him.

Beefy rubbed his chin as he watched the guys resume their training, now with more gusto. 'I want a promotion,' he declared.

'Oh, do you?'

'Yep. I want to be Chief Motivational Officer.'

'Mate,' I said, 'the job's yours.'

It turned out Beefy wasn't only good at pulling a team out of a slump; he knew how to keep egos in check, too. A year or so later, Melbourne University came into some good form; we won three games in a row and all four grades were up around the top of the ladder. Training was a hoot; we were prancing about like peacocks. There was joy at every turn.

At the end of one session we all confidently cruised over to Beefy for his weekly motivational address, and he didn't hesitate to mow us all down.

'Hey boys, how do you reckon you're going?' he said, looking around at all the smug faces. 'Do you reckon you're going alright? Well you might be, but fucking get over yourselves! I'm fucking sick of you boys strutting around like you own the joint. Just fucking get over yourselves.' Then he walked off.

Honestly, who else could give us the truth like that?

Beefy still gives the boys a motivational speech in a huddle every Thursday night. Most of the time he yells and swears at us but he always has a message, even if it's delivered in footy clichés. Often they're brilliant, often they're insightful, and sometimes they give us new perspective on what it means to be thankful for what you've got.

Beefy had first come into my life as I was working hard to practise the principles I'd learned in India and share them with my students at SEDA. I strongly believed that gratitude, empathy and mindfulness – GEM, in shorthand – were the foundations of a happier life.

Beefy, however, had taught me something just as powerful. Through my connection with him, I'd navigated my way through an awful breakup and the loss of my granny. The very act of reaching out to Beefy, and offering him relationships beyond what he had experienced before, brought home a huge lesson in my life: the power of personal connection. I would soon find out just how crucial to our happiness that can be.

CHAPTER 6
IN MEMORY OF LUKE

Properly scoring a cricket match is near impossible. It is for me, anyway. I've been playing my whole life and I still can't get my head around the mind-boggling complexity of the scorebook. Just the sight of one makes me break out in a cold sweat. Thank God we had Luke.

Luke was an excellent scorer and a valued member of the Melbourne University Cricket Club. He also happened to be autistic. MUCC had an association with Autism Australia and, from time to time, we would advertise through them: 'Anyone who loves numbers and loves cricket, please get in touch because we're looking for scorers.'

Luke answered the call. He was a quiet man in his early forties, and he struggled socially. It was hard watching the anxiety overtake him when he was around other people; at times it was almost crippling for him. But Luke committed to the club regardless. I instantly loved him – our whole club did – because he cared passionately about scoring cricket.

So devoted was Luke that he'd stress out about being late to the games, and would do trial runs during the week. He would drive to the grounds we were scheduled to play at, to gauge how long it would take him to get there on game day.

Luke had a job packing shelves at Coles from 4.30 until 6.30 am. He kept himself busy during the rest of the day with delivering newspapers, field-umpiring football and working at a Vinnies store. He also found time to do home-to-oval time trials through the suburbs of Melbourne in the lead-up to our cricket matches. As a result he was only ever late once, though it upset him badly. 'Luke, it's fine,' I assured him when he arrived a whole 22 minutes late. 'We're batting. We've got your back – one of the boys is on the book. You're here now, and that's all that matters.'

'No, it's not fine,' Luke said.

'Yeah, really it's fine, mate. So what happened anyway?'

'The Navman fucked me!' he spat. Luke never swore, so I knew how shattered and furious he was that technology had let him down. His uncharacteristically vulgar outburst was met with uproarious laughter from the whole team, and a few of the boys patted him on the back. He looked a little confused, but joined in laughing anyway.

Luke became a beloved fixture at the club and he loved the club right back. He always joined the players in the change room after the game; we'd hand him a can of Coke, which he'd typically skol in one go. Having demolished his drink, he'd just sit there with a big smile on his face.

Because of his social anxiety, Luke tended to stay off to the side in the change rooms. Sometimes we'd succeed in beckoning him to join in with the boys. He thought it was great – a privilege – but it clearly made him nervous and before long he'd stand up, announce, 'I've got to go!' and head out the door.

One day we enjoyed a particularly close victory and the boys were ecstatic afterwards. We pulled Luke into the group, handed him his Coke, rubbed his hair and treated him just like everyone else in what Beefy called the 'inner sanctum'. Luke handled it as best he could but after a couple of minutes, just like clockwork, he rose to his feet and declared, 'I've got to go.'

When he reached the door, however, Luke turned to face us all and said, 'I have an announcement to make.'

'Oh yeah, Lukey? What is it?'

'The announcement is that you guys are my best friends.' Then he turned as red as a cricket ball and ran to his car.

In one of Luke's first outings as scorer, I was sitting next to him and admiring his work with the scorebook. I noticed he was taking a keen interest in my MUCC T-shirt and, sure enough, he soon asked where he could get one.

'I've got a spare in my car, mate,' I said. 'I'll give it to you after the game.' He looked overjoyed.

After the game, I was giving the customary captain's summary when I remembered my promise to Luke. Someone discreetly gave me the T-shirt then I said to the group, 'And now for something special. We are so lucky to have Luke scoring for us. He's a great bloke, and we love him dearly.'

Luke knew exactly what was going on! He marched straight up to the front and stood next to me before I even had a chance to explain to the group what I was presenting. Just like that, Luke took his shirt off and threw it to the side. He stood there topless, hands on his hips, waiting for the shirt to be presented. It was hard not to laugh at such a wonderful display of enthusiasm.

'So, Lukey, it's a great pleasure to present you with your own club T-shirt.' He put it on instantly and stood in front of the group with the biggest of smiles.

Moments later, when the applause had died down, I leant over towards Luke and invited him to join a bunch of us for dinner that night. We were going to his favourite pub.

'I can't,' he said. 'I'm going to Mum and Dad's house to show 'em my new T-shirt.'

And that was Luke, through and through.

Over time Luke loosened up as much as his autism would allow him to, and one day he even cracked a joke. We were sitting around during a lunch break and for some reason I was telling a ghost story. All the while, Luke just sat there, staring intently at me.

'Do you believe in ghosts, Lukey?' I asked.

'Yep, yep, I've seen ghosts actually,' he replied.

'What?!' we all inquired at once.

'Yep, I see them all the time.'

'Do they scare you?' I asked.

'Nah, they're not scary once you've seen them,' he assured us. 'They don't move very fast.'

'So where did you see these ghosts, Lukey?' we all wanted to know.

'In paddocks,' he said, smiling, 'where they belong. So yeah, I believe in goats.'

Goats! The whole team lost it, and our response left Luke in no doubt that he'd nailed it. He kept the smile on his face for the rest of the day.

Luke was a wizard with numbers and statistics, and he'd developed his own colour-coded system for scoring. One day he left his coloured pencils in his car, so I volunteered to go and get them so he could keep his eye on the game. When I unlocked Luke's car I was surprised to see 20 or 30 DVDs scattered across the back seat.

'Hey Lukey,' I said when I returned and handed him the pencils, 'can I take a guess at your favourite movie of all time?'

'Sure,' he said. 'Go ahead.'

'I reckon your favourite movie is *When Harry Met Sally*.'

'Yes!' he said. 'How did you know that?'

'Do you like *Notting Hill* as well?'

'Yes, that's also my favourite!'

'Gee, I'm good at guessing,' I said, and listed another half-dozen of the romantic comedies Luke had stockpiled in his car.

'How do you know all this?' he demanded.

'I just saw them in the back of your car, mate! What's going on there?'

'They're my favourites, Hughey, so I take them everywhere with me.'

Honestly, he was one of the most beautiful people I'd ever had the good fortune of meeting.

Since cricket and scoring were a massive part of Luke's life, he seemed to struggle a bit in the off-season, when all the stumps and bats and balls disappear from suburban ovals. You can't score training sessions, so Luke was always anxious for the next season to roll around ASAP. I knew this because, without fail, he would phone me on the first of June every year:

'Hughey, it's Lukey. How long until the cricket season starts?'

'There's four months to go, mate,' I'd say.

'Oh, that's a long time. Bye.' Then he'd hang up without another word.

On the first of July he'd ring again.

'Hughey, it's Lukey.'

'I know mate, I've got caller ID. I know when it's you!'

'How long until the cricket season starts?'

'Three months, Lukey. Getting closer.'

'Oh, that's a long time. Bye.'

It went like this on the first of every month, right through the off-season, until it was 'cricket time' again. A few years ago Luke called me in mid-September and said, 'Hughey, how long until cricket starts?'

'Mate, it's only a couple of weeks away now,' I replied. 'Sharpen those pencils, brother!'

There was a long pause at the other end of the line before Luke finally said, 'That still feels like a long time to me.' Then he fell silent again. And he hung up without another word.

Something was a bit off about the phone call, but I figured he was probably fine. It was a bit of an awkward call and I didn't want to just come out and ask him if he was alright. I figured his autism might have been blurring the communication a little, so I just hung up without probing how he was feeling or if he was OK.

Four days later I got a phone call from the club president to let me know that Luke had taken his own life.

A week later, 35 young men turned up to farewell Luke at his funeral. His parents and siblings were blown away that so many people had felt the impact of his loss so deeply; that these young cricketers cared so much about their Luke.

'Are you serious?' I said to them. 'Everyone loved Luke. We absolutely loved him.'

That day Luke's brother delivered the most heart-wrenching eulogy. It still makes me cry when I think about it.

'I decided to go for a walk the other day to work out what I was going to say in a eulogy for Luke,' his brother said. 'I was walking beside the river and I saw a group of ducks paddling upstream. Even though I knew the ducks were working hard under the surface, I found myself admiring how effortless they made it look as they glided across the water.

'My attention was pulled towards a solitary duck that was a few metres behind the group, battling away, trying hard to keep up with the others. As hard as this duck was trying, it just couldn't catch up with them.'

He paused for a long time as tears flooded down his cheeks. 'And that was Luke,' he finally said, choking on the words. 'It was just so hard for him to keep up. But Luke, you don't need to work that hard anymore, mate. Your struggles are over.'

We'll never know why the world became too much for Luke to bear. I do know that he lived for the cricket season. It was one of his great passions and, on the face of it, maybe having to wait two more weeks for the season to start again was two weeks too much. I really just don't know.

We don't have many pictures on the wall at Melbourne University Cricket Club. We've had some legends of the game go on to play for Australia, but a photo of Luke has pride of place on the change-room wall, and we still talk about him all the time. Sometimes the younger players will ask who he is and I love being able to tell them.

Luke's story underscores the need to not only make connections but to make them count. On that September day four years ago I had the opportunity to ask Luke if he was OK emotionally and I didn't. I know things can get awkward, especially between men:

'He's probably fine!'

'He's probably just distracted!'

'It's none of my business!'

'What if I ask him if he's OK and he *is* OK, but then he thinks that I think he's being weird?'

We can always find a reason to not ask someone if they're OK. My last conversation with Luke was a reminder that you never know what's going on in someone else's life, and if you're not sure, it's best to just ask them.

You can always use the standard line 'Are you OK?' or you can say, 'How are you travelling? Do you want to have a beer? Or a coffee? Or go for a walk?' Having friendships is wonderful, but sometimes we need to create the opportunities to truly care for one another; to be there in the thick of it when the friendship needs it most.

Like Luke, I've always loved cricket. I'm still competitive, but truth be told I'm not overly worried about how many wins and losses we have these days. When I look back on my time in cricket, it's not the premierships I think about; it's the lasting personal connections and friendships I've made. Sometimes we can be easily distracted by the small things in life, but we have been put on Earth to connect with others, to be there for one another. I wish I'd been there for Luke – and I'll do everything I can to ensure I don't make that mistake again.

CHAPTER 7

MINUS ONE COFFEE

I started putting the lessons I'd learned in India about gratitude, empathy and mindfulness into practice at SEDA, the school where I met Beefy. We used sport as a vehicle to educate kids; naturally that was a good fit for me, and I found it to be a great environment in which to weave the three principles of wellbeing into my teaching.

The boys at SEDA were the first male students I had taught for any meaningful length of time. I'd been on a learning curve with the tweenage girls at Fintona, but the boys – I just got them straight away. Especially Beefy. Young men need to know that you care about them. My experience with them bore out the expression, 'Students won't care how much you know until they know how much you care.' So I let them know I cared. I hadn't long been drawing upon the principles of GEM – gratitude, empathy and mindfulness – but I managed to embed them into our lessons at every opportunity.

GRATITUDE

One thing I often did was single out a student and launch into a spiel about why I was so grateful to have them in the class; modelling good behaviour is the most powerful way to encourage that behaviour in others. The easiest way to introduce daily gratitude practice into their lives, however, came at leaving time: I would often stand at the door and ask them to tell me three good things from their day before they went home.

Once a term, I put pieces of butcher's paper on the classroom walls, each with the name of a student as the heading, then I would ask everyone to go around and write down why they were grateful to have that person in our class. It was so rewarding to see the students take their piece of paper down at the end of the session – pretending, of course, that they weren't overly interested in what was on it – then study it closely, trying hard not to smile.

EMPATHY

Random acts of kindness were a huge part of the classroom experience. I would ask the students to come and tell me in private when they had done something kind for someone else. I would then send an email to their parents, copying in the student, letting them know how kind their child had been. Apart from one dad, who asked me to 'stop sending these weird emails', the parents loved it – and, in turn, the students were motivated to look out for other people.

We integrated bigger acts of kindness into our routine, too. There was one student who was going through a bit of a rough patch at home, so one day when he wasn't at school I called an emergency 'team' meeting with the rest of the class. Everyone was asked to come up with a suggestion for what we could do to make this kid smile the next time he came to school.

The plan we settled on was simple: this student *loved* his footy, but he often struggled to get a kick during our biweekly inter-class matches, so we orchestrated a game where he could kick six goals. The next time we played, I put this boy at full forward, and the plan went off without a hitch. I'd never seen him smile like that before, and his happiness was infectious. The other students couldn't stop smiling and asking him about his miraculous performance.

MINDFULNESS

I started each day by having the students walk a lap of the sports fields before coming into class, where they had to write down five things they heard, saw and felt on the walk. Although they found the exercise tedious at first, after a couple of months they genuinely looked forward to it. The exercise called to mind Stanzin and his classmates attending their optional half-hour of meditation each morning.

Over the first year I watched carefully to see what impact the daily practice of gratitude, empathy and mindfulness had on the kids. It was profound. My major observation was that these kids walked taller.

A big part of this turnaround was also SEDA's focus on engaging students and measuring them by their talents rather than objective curriculum standards of literacy and numeracy (although there was still plenty of that). Their healthy self-esteem would, I hope, help to safeguard them from the perils of the brutal adolescent years.

While I felt I was definitely onto something, I was pretty much flying by the seat of my pants. I had no research to back up my instincts that these simple skills were essential for kids to become happier. It was time I got busy.

In 2010 I commenced studying part time for my Master of Education at RMIT. The course offered a lot of autonomy, so I had the latitude to structure my learning around student mental health and wellbeing. If I was given an assignment examining 'issues among international students', for example, I would hone my approach accordingly. If I was asked to explore student assessments, I would look at assessments of student wellbeing. Over the following four and a half years I essentially designed my own bespoke master's degree in education, focusing on adolescent and child wellbeing.

The more I studied, the clearer it became that the time to act on wellbeing was long overdue. One early assignment required me to research and deliver a two-hour-long presentation on the topic of 'contemporary issues in education'. I could not think of a more pressing issue than the mental health of the students we were teaching. The problem wasn't that schools weren't active in the area, it was that, for whatever reasons, the approaches they were taking weren't making a significant impact on a diabolically grim situation.

World Health Organization figures show we in the West are more depressed, less connected, more anxious and more likely to die by suicide than ever before in recorded history. Across every metric, the figures are chilling. In the most recent National Health Survey, from the period 2017–18, one in five Australians – that's a whopping 4.8 million people – reported a mental or behavioural condition, an increase of 2.6 per cent from 2014–15.[1] Roughly one in eight Australians aged 18 and over experienced high or very high levels of psychological distress in that period.[2]

Having lived through the consequences of 'very high levels of psychological distress' on a family, I knew those figures didn't reflect the concentric circles of suffering that ripple outwards and touch brothers and sisters, mums and dads, aunties and uncles and friends.

I thought a lot about Georgia during that time, and what she'd been through. Surely there had to be some kind of antidote to all the suffering we endure? Or if not an antidote, then a way to help us better weather the storms when the dark clouds gather and the winds of ill fortune blow.

◾

One of the first things I studied was gratitude. When I read the work of renowned American psychologist Martin Seligman, I nearly fell off my chair. Widely known as the founder of positive psychology, Dr Seligman showed that we can, in effect, retrain our brains so we feel happier on a day-to-day basis.

In a classic study that's been cited more than 6000 times,[3] Dr Seligman and other leading researchers described a simple technique: to write down three things that went well each day, every day, along with an explanation for why each good thing happened. It's been shown that when human beings take time to look for and cogitate on the good things that happen to them every day, after one month our brains start scanning the world for positives rather than negatives.

Participants in the study also conducted a 'gratitude visit', in which they were given one week to write then deliver in person a letter of gratitude to someone who had been kind to them but never properly thanked. This group showed improved mood and fewer symptoms of depression almost immediately, as well as up to one month after the visit. Dr Seligman found that, over the medium to long term, practising these 'gratitude interventions' made people happier overall.

Studies have long shown human beings are more likely to register a greater psychological impact from a negative experience than a positive experience. It's known as 'the negativity bias', and while it may have resulted from mankind's evolutionary need to be alert to threats and predators, these days the bias poses one of the biggest challenges to dealing with mental health: we are wired to be seduced by the negative.

Dr Seligman's research chimed with my experiences in India. I had seen Stanzin routinely accentuate the positives in his daily life, only Stanzin went one step further – he noted these in the moment. He didn't have a pen to write them down, let alone a phone to type into. Instead, Stanzin literally stopped what he was doing and pointed to whatever he was grateful for in any given moment: 'Dis!'

There's one word that sums up Stanzin's process: gratitude.

Over the past few decades, as more and more research has been done in the area, studies have indicated associations between practising gratitude and improvements in emotional wellbeing, fewer symptoms of stress, anxiety and depression, higher levels of self-esteem, enhanced life satisfaction, better quality of life and greater optimism.[4] Within the context of work, gratitude has been shown to correlate with greater personal accomplishment, job satisfaction, work wellbeing and reduced burnout.[5]

If we could teach children how to practise gratitude and get them to actively take note of three things they were thankful for each day, I realised, then we would have a better chance at turning the tide of anxiety and depression that was creeping up and up and up in the statistics.

Although I loved Dr Seligman's strategy of recording what went well at the end of a day, I preferred Stanzin's approach of recording these things in the moment. 'How good is this?' I would think to myself in moments of reflection. 'How good is playing cricket on a beautiful Saturday afternoon? Enjoying a quiet coffee in my favourite cafe? Spending time with Mum and Dad?' Always with Stanzin's voice in the back of my mind: 'How good is dis?'

Not long after I'd returned from India I got chatting with one of my ex-colleagues at Fintona about my experiences on the subcontinent.

'You should come in one day and give a talk to my class,' she offered.

A week later I was back in front of the girls I'd taught a year earlier. I armed myself with photos from my time in India: the school on the edge of the desert, the busted play equipment and, of course, little Stanzin. I hadn't prepared what I was going to say; I just hoped to illustrate the ways the kids in northern India experienced school as opposed to the Fintona girls with their beautiful facilities.

I told them how the kids in the Indian school had to sit on a dirt floor during lessons. I told them how the students meditated for half an hour before school each day, even though it wasn't compulsory. I found myself telling them a lot about Stanzin – the kindest person I had ever met – and how he epitomised the resilience and abundant happiness that the people of his village possessed in spite of their poverty, which was in such stark contrast to the leafy and affluent eastern suburbs of Melbourne.

The story was a lot for the girls of an elite Western private school to take in. Gauging from the absolute silence in the room and the wide-eyed looks on their faces when I finished, they *really* took it in. Afterwards some of the girls made a point of telling me how 'awesome' the talk had been, and how it made them realise for the first time how good we have it in Australia.

'That's where gratitude begins,' I told them. 'It's about focusing on the things we have, not the things we don't have. If you're able to do that all the time, you're going to be much happier in life.'

I was buoyed by their response, as well as my own

reaction to the talk. Though I'd never done anything like it before, I discovered I loved sharing such a positive message with children. As a teacher I knew how to get their attention with an engaging story and then use that to drive home the important lessons, which I'd intuitively understood at first, based on my experiences in early life and in India, but which were increasingly being confirmed by the research I was studying:

PRACTISE GRATITUDE: FOCUS ON THE POSITIVES AND THE THINGS YOU HAVE

Seligman's well-known study of the positive effects of 'gratitude interventions' was backed up by another couple of studies I was later drawn to. The practice of writing and delivering gratitude letters was shown in a 2012 study to generate higher levels of happiness and life satisfaction, and fewer symptoms of depression in participants. The letter-writers were asked to be reflective and write their letters expressively, and that positive orientation lifted their indicators of wellbeing.[6]

A 2015 study looked at the impact of writing in a gratitude diary three times a week for two weeks. Even after that small timeframe, these participants exhibited an increased sense of optimism and fewer signs of emotional distress.[7]

CULTIVATE EMPATHY: BE KIND TO OTHERS

The research was likewise pretty clear on the benefits of acting kindly and with compassion towards others. This could be as simple as listening to a member of a marginalised or stigmatised group, which can lead to more positive attitudes towards them,[8] or practising a form of meditation that focuses on empathy and compassion. In one 2013 study, participants engaged in a compassion-based meditation once a week for eight weeks, after which they were unwittingly part of a set-up in which an actor on crutches would walk into the waiting room they were in. Participants who had engaged in the meditation were more likely to offer their seat to the 'sufferer' than those in the control group, leading the researchers to link this meditation to an increased likelihood of acting to relieve another person's suffering.[9]

There's also been a lot of research recently on the impact of 'acts of kindness': brief, one-time, 'pay it forward'–style activities like offering to help someone carry something, giving a compliment or even giving gifts. In one study, participants were asked to complete a 14-day diary that listed five of these acts they engaged in each day – that is, they were asked to both commit kindness and count kindness.[10] The results were pretty common across the board: significant increases in several aspects of wellbeing, including optimism and life satisfaction, a decrease in symptoms of anxiety, and even a greater sense of connectedness and peer acceptance.[11]

BE MINDFUL: TAKE TIME TO FOCUS ON THE PRESENT MOMENT

For me, this was a crucial point when it came to dealing with the ever-creeping statistics on youth and adolescent stress, anxiety and depression. Some studies took place over a short-term period like eight weeks, and even within that timeframe, participants who engaged in weekly meditation sessions felt lower levels of stress and exhaustion, and higher quality of life.[12] In one study that took place across five schools, students were led through guided weekly mindfulness exercises (such as mindful breathing and body scans), shared their meditation experiences and reflection in small groups, and were assigned daily homework to reflect on their meditation and reading. After six months, the students who engaged in mindfulness practice demonstrated significantly greater reductions in depressive symptoms than the control group.[13] The longer-term impacts were further supported by a study in which participants showed increased wellbeing after sticking with mindfulness sessions in some capacity over a six-year period.[14]

As I increased my research into GEM principles during my master's degree, I started to think I could share this message with other students. It was the first step on a long road that would eventually lead to the creation of what I called The Resilience Project.

Soon after the talk at Fintona, I received an invitation from a nearby high school to speak to the students. I managed to hold the attention of 380 teenagers for four hours' worth of content. It was another indication that the message was landing well with kids. I felt I might be on the right track.

University, cricket and work already soaked up a lot of my time, so there wasn't much room left in the day to put a huge effort into developing a program for my school talks. Further troubled by the research and statistics about mental illness I read each year, in 2011 I decided to leap into the deep end and give it my all. I left my job at SEDA to throw everything I had at getting The Resilience Project off the ground.

It wasn't called that back then; the name went through a few different iterations before I settled on it. The operative word was always 'resilience', though: I'd always felt, in my time as a teacher, that resilience was the most important life skill a child needed in order to learn and grow. I knew from my firsthand observations and my research that a resilient child – and the resilient adult they would become – is less likely to bully and be bullied, less likely to develop mental health issues, and would be generally better equipped to deal with life's curve balls.

I delivered the talk to my old school, Carey Baptist Grammar, which went down well. As my confidence grew I contacted other schools and arranged to sit down with principals and leading teachers to see if they were interested. I wasn't charging much – just enough to cover my petrol and help pay my rent, because I was sharing a house in Fitzroy with two of my best friends, a mate from cricket and his then girlfriend. I wasn't thinking about money; my main motive was to help kids be happier. The more I read about gratitude, empathy and mindfulness and the more I practised these principles myself, the more they became my main motivation for getting out of bed every day.

For every small step forward, however, I took at least one step back.

'Have you done this talk before?' principals would invariably ask when they met me.

'Yes, I've done it at my old school and the girls' school I used to teach at,' I'd respond.

'Maybe you should come back to us next year, when you've got a few more runs on the board.'

So much for being on my way. For a long time hardly anyone wanted to hear the presentation. I kept putting myself forward but being knocked back. Before long, I had to start working again as an emergency teacher, which was a tough pill to swallow – but a necessary one in order to keep me and the project afloat. Every once in a while, though, a school would book me to give a talk, which kept my motivation and my spirits up, and helped pay a few bills along the way.

After 18 months, things started to look a bit dire on the financial front. I'd wake up early every day and drive to my favourite cafe in Fitzroy because we had no mobile reception at the share house. I'd sit at the cafe and wait for the phone to ring with offers of emergency teaching work and – fingers crossed – a school that was interested in The Resilience Project. Outside in the car I had my suit (in case I got a call to teach at a private school), jeans and a collared shirt (in case I was working at a public school), plus my sports gear should I end up teaching PE for the day.

I was hunkered down in the cafe as usual at 6 am one day, willing the phone to vibrate into life with an offer of work. When, after three hours, no one had called, I ordered a coffee and slumped back into my chair, feeling flat. I finished my strong latte and walked to the counter to pay.

When I swiped my card in the EFTPOS machine the little screen issued a cold, humiliating message: 'Insufficient funds.'

The waitress made a slightly annoyed, slightly pitying face. 'The coffee is four dollars,' she reminded me. To most of her customers four bucks was chickenfeed, but to me it felt like I was being asked to pay off the national debt.

'Ah, look, I'll just pop out to the car and grab some coins,' I told her. 'Back in a sec.'

Two minutes later I returned, sheepish. 'I actually don't have any money in the car.' I chuckled self-consciously. 'I live around the corner. I've got some coins at home – I'll be back.'

Fifteen minutes later I returned to the cafe counter.

'I'm really sorry,' I told the unsmiling waitress, 'but I've got no money at home either.'

'Well, we don't give out free coffees here,' she said, plunging a coffee stirrer through my already wounded heart. I promised I'd return later with the four dollars, and shamefully slunk back out the door.

So there I was, standing on a footpath in Fitzroy at the age of 31 with a university education, qualifications to teach, a master's degree from RMIT on the boil . . . and a total wealth of minus one coffee.

'I can't keep doing this,' I said as I regaled my housemates with the coffee tragedy that night. 'I have to get back into teaching. I'm just going to have to stop with these talks.'

To their everlasting credit, my housemates proved they were great mates to have in a crisis. 'Don't be silly, Hugh!' they said. 'You've got this. It will work! What you're doing is really special.' They insisted on paying my rent for the next month and I took my rental bond money out, which they covered too.

Even though I had a little more breathing room, life became one long groundhog day. A couple more schools asked me to give the resilience talk to their students but, for the most part, I sat around waiting for the phone to ring, or chased my tail doing emergency teaching. Before long,

I was dangerously close to the breadline again – or the coffee line, as it were. 'Honestly, guys, I can't keep doing this,' I told my housemates again. 'I'll have to go back into teaching full time.'

A week later my phone rang and when I picked up, a panicked-sounding woman started talking. She was calling from a conference room in Ararat, west of Melbourne. 'It's a gathering of principals, and our guest speaker has just cancelled at the last minute,' she said. 'I've heard that you do talks. I don't know what you talk about, but someone has said you give presentations. Can you get here within an hour?'

'No,' I replied, 'but I can get there in an hour and a half.'

'We'll take it,' she said.

I hung up, grabbed my laptop and jumped in the car. As I drove to the venue I kept thinking, 'This is it – make or break. I'm going to have fifty principals in a room. If they connect with the talk, this could be huge. If they don't connect, I'm done.'

Ever since I'd given my first talk to the girls at Fintona, I'd worked hard to make sure the presentation had undeniable emotional impact so that the accompanying message about the importance of practising gratitude, empathy and mindfulness would stick.

The talk revolved around two key stories. The first was about my experiences in India and the things I learned from Stanzin. The second, which I didn't like to tell so much but was absolutely necessary, was the story of how mental illness had ravaged my little sister, and the rest of my family along with her. I had asked Georgia if she minded that I shared her life's nadir with strangers. 'If it helps someone else,' she said, 'I'm all for it.'

Within two days of speaking at the principals' conference, 48 out of the 50 schools represented there asked me to give the resilience talk to their students. Suddenly I was booked for a year. The Resilience Project was still just centred on me giving talks, but some of the school representatives asked, 'It's a program, isn't it? It's an ongoing program for the whole year?'

'Yes, definitely,' I responded.

'Do you talk about leadership as well?'

'Yep, sure,' I said. 'It's mainly about resilience, but I can talk about leadership.'

I was stretching things a little but I knew I needed to get my foot in the door, get access to these thousands of kids and give them the tools that would help strengthen them against the plague of depression and anxiety in the community. *Then* I could think about a 'program'.

Life began to get very hectic. I went from sitting around in cafes, not being able to pay for coffee, to wondering how I was ever going to service all those schools. It turned out to be the perfect time to be single.

I put everything into building and managing The Resilience Project. Over the following year I presented at dozens of schools throughout Victoria. In my spare time I plugged away at my Master of Education and researched anything I could find on adolescent mental health.

As I'd suspected, the need for education on mental health and wellbeing was dire. The most recent data we have from the Australian Bureau of Statistics, from 2017, shows that 98 children, defined as aged between five and 17, died by suicide in that year, the leading cause of death for that age group and a 10.1 per cent increase in deaths from the previous year.[15] Tracing that statistic alone is nothing short of horrifying.

One in seven children and adolescents experiences poor mental health, which translates to tens of thousands of school students around Australia, but a 2015 Australian Government report found that only one in four of those with mental health problems had attended professional services in the six months before the survey.[16] I made a personal promise to do my best to help these children and young people.

At each talk I delivered, there'd be at least one teacher who knew a teacher at another school. Thanks to this word-of-mouth chain, it wasn't long before I was speaking at ten schools a week – a clear sign that teachers were identifying a desperate need for GEM to be taught in our schools.

I'd give presentations during the day, then go home and try to do the invoicing, reply to emails that were flooding in from schools and organise the bookings so none of them missed out. Soon enough, I started getting inquiries from interstate: 'My friend just saw you do this presentation. I'm a teacher at a state school in Queensland. Do you do talks up here?'

With no accountancy training or any idea whatsoever about the operational side of things, I was suddenly trying to manage a rapidly expanding business. I had never conceived of The Resilience Project as a 'business' as such – it was simply a vehicle for me to fulfil my purpose. That sense of purpose had only been further clarified and sharpened by my experiences in schools around the state: make as many people as possible feel happier.

Nevertheless, a business is what The Resilience Project became – and I proved to be a hopeless businessman. I lost track of paperwork, I was just as likely to forget to send an invoice as to remember, and I said yes to virtually everything, travelling just about anywhere no matter how fatigued it left me.

I'll never forget one of the most hectic two-day periods from that time. During the first morning I delivered three one-hour sessions back-to-back at a primary school in Melbourne, then I got in the car and drove to Portland, four and a half hours away, where I delivered a teacher training session followed by a talk with a community group. Immediately after, I drove back to Melbourne that night as I had to present at a school first thing the next morning. All up, it was nine hours of driving for five hours of presenting. I sometimes look back and wonder how I survived such days. Yet while I was the most sleep deprived I had ever been, I was also the most fulfilled.

It wasn't only the number of bookings that made me realise I was helping people; I could also perceive this from the looks on the kids' faces and the tone of their voices when I had conversations with them afterwards. The feedback from teachers was just as positive: evidence that the stories I told were having an impact on adults as well as children. Many teachers encouraged me to expand The Resilience Project to include seminars for parents as well. Parents needed this message more than anyone, they would say.

It became clear that people wanted more than to hear

me talk about my experiences and summarise all the neuro-scientific research into the benefits of GEM. I was also being asked by schools to create a curriculum, again and again. I loved that idea. I knew that if I genuinely wanted to change behaviours and make a dent in the mental health crisis, I couldn't just swan up to a school, do a talk then leave. Ongoing support for teachers via a year-long curriculum was a fantastic idea.

I invested all the money we had made from the talks in the development of a comprehensive curriculum: 30 lessons for every year level, from prep/kindergarten to Year 12. The lessons were written by teachers for teachers, and in addition to structured lessons on GEM we included lessons on emotional literacy (how students could better communicate their feelings). You cannot understate how important it is for people to be able to identify and label their emotions, and put into words why they feel those emotions. We also produced 21-day and six-month wellbeing journals for adults.

Considering the excellent standard of living in Australia, why were the figures around depression, social anxiety and youth suicide staying the same, if not getting worse? One likely factor was the de-stigmatisation of mental illness over the previous 20 years, which had led to an increase in people willing to report problems. But another more insidious reason was the impact that smartphones and social media were having on the social landscape. This revolution in technology and human interaction was supposed to bring the world closer together. In some ways it was pushing people – children and adolescents particularly – further and further apart.

By the end of 2014, The Resilience Project had been adopted into 500 public, private and independent schools across the country. I had spoken to tens of thousands of primary and secondary students, along with their parents and teachers. It was just the beginning of our journey as an organisation: by early 2019, our schools program manager and my dear friend Antony informed me that within that year alone we would have 110,000 kids around the country involved with our curriculum or presentations.

It was hard not to be emotional when I considered how far I had come. I remembered the joy and fulfilment I had felt when I'd finished my first presentation to a class of twenty girls. It was mind-blowing to realise we'd since reached so many kids around the country, and they'd been taught how to practise GEM principles every day. The statistics around mental illness are frightening, and it's my hope that The Resilience Project can play a small part in helping to turn the tide on the mental health epidemic still looming over the nation's children.

CHAPTER 8

A FILE CALLED REGRET

When I was in Years 7 and 8, I was obsessed with only one thing outside of cricket: Sarah James, the most beautiful girl at Carey Baptist Grammar. Since I was inwardly shy, I felt some discomfort along with the excitement that comes with a teenage crush. Sarah was a shimmering distant moon on the other side of the playground, and I knew that if I wanted any form of communication with her I would have to go and stand in front of her, talk to her and pray a swarm of butterflies didn't fly out of my mouth. It was a horrifying prospect.

After geeing myself up for several weeks, I somehow got the nerve to do it. Never had I felt so terrified, so vulnerable or so excited as when I stepped towards Sarah one lunchtime, like Neil Armstrong, and threw myself at the universe.

'Ah, hi Sarah!' I said and smiled at her.

'Hi Hugh!' she answered and smiled right back. We struck up a proper conversation from there.

My relief and elation were off the charts. I had been dreading rejection but I was so glad I'd gone through with it. Sarah and I shared a few classes so we got to talking some more, then we hung out together in groups of our friends, but if I wanted to go a step further and have a private conversation with her I knew I would have to steel myself for another conquest. To take our relationship beyond the orbit of school I had to find the intestinal fortitude to pick up the phone, call her home number – knowing her mum or dad would answer – and say, 'Hi Mr/Mrs James, this is Hugh van Cuylenburg. I go to school with Sarah. I was wondering if I could please speak with her.'

At 13, *that* took courage. But having to talk directly to one of her folks was just the beginning of the fraught business of calling Sarah at home. Once I'd cleared the parental gatekeepers I had to move quickly onto stage two – actually having a worthwhile phone conversation with the most beautiful girl in the world. To prepare myself I'd write a running sheet of topics to discuss so we didn't drift into an awkward silence. A typical list would read:

- Funny story about a teacher
- How's netball going?
- How's tennis going?
- Why do you reckon backhand is so much harder than forehand?
- What racquet do you use?
- My parents are so annoying (mine weren't, but this is something every teenager seems to say at some point).
- Cute story about my little brother

This was hardly pioneering. Millions of kids around the world no doubt did the same thing. These phone calls were a rite of passage; they were how we learned the skills necessary to interact and communicate well with others, including adults, and to make connections.

By Year 12 I'd fallen madly in love with another girl, Christie, who'd arrived at our school a year earlier. I will never forget the feeling of properly falling in love for the first time; that feeling seemed to elevate every waking moment.

Christie was the quintessential girl next door, even though she had grown up anything but next door. Her family lived out of town on a couple of hundred acres. Mobile phones hadn't quite become ubiquitous in 1998 so, once again, if I wanted to talk to Christie outside of school I had to call her at home, which I did almost every night without fail. More than two decades later, I can still recite her home phone number.

Christie's dad was an engineer who mostly worked from home, so the home phone number was essentially his office line, too. Nine times out of ten it was he who answered whenever I called. Before long we started having long conversations that would sometimes last ten to 15 minutes before I'd get around to asking if Christie was free.

Christie's dad loved his sport and was always interested in how I was going at cricket and football – so much so that he'd even come and watch me play on the weekends. I was 17 turning 18 and he was approaching 50, but by talking on the phone almost every day we developed a wonderful friendship. More than once we got so caught up in conversation I'd say goodbye and hang up, having completely forgotten to speak with Christie. Sometimes I would hear Christie in the background, yelling, 'Dad, he didn't call to speak to you!'

It was from this man that I learned to take an interest in others – a real interest. Most times when I asked how things were going in his life, he'd turn the conversation back to me: 'No, no, nothing much interesting to tell you, Hugh. Now what's the latest with your cricket? How's your mum and dad? Tell me how things are going at school.'

Christie's dad taught me that being genuinely interested in other people is how you connect and develop strong, lasting relationships. If you don't really care what's going on in someone's life, you're never going to be close with them. I also learned from him not to talk about myself all the time; everybody's life is interesting, and the more you listen the quicker you learn that we all have a story.

Sadly, at the time, I didn't exactly apply those lessons to the people I loved most in the world, partly because we can take our families for granted and partly because I wanted to escape the misery of mine. Georgia's anorexia had pulled her into a downward spiral that was gradually widening to grab hold of all of us. As I recounted in Chapter 1, I refused to properly acknowledge her mental illness, and I hated seeing Mum and Dad in so much pain and watching my poor brother Josh struggle. After I graduated from high school I spent an increasing amount of time at Christie's place, where I bonded even more with her dad.

Eventually Christie and I drifted apart and filled our lives with other people, but I often thought about her dad. About two years later, one of my childhood dreams was on the verge of coming true: my Melbourne University cricket team made the district grand final, which was going to be played upon the hallowed turf of the Melbourne Cricket Ground. I knew Christie's dad would have been thrilled for me, so I called him up to share the news.

He was in the crowd a few weeks later when I strode into the middle of the MCG and steamed in off the long run. That day I trod in the footsteps of my boyhood heroes Steve Waugh, Craig McDermott and Ricky Ponting, and virtually every other great player in the history of cricket.

We chatted after the match and I asked how Christie was. Then I asked him how he was doing. 'No, no, Hugh, nothing interesting going on,' he said, putting a hand on my shoulder and smiling widely. 'Tell me, what was it like to play at The G?' As usual, he was more interested in the person he was with.

It was the last time I spoke to him face-to-face. Bone marrow cancer took him very quickly two years later. I was unprepared for how much I cried at his funeral.

■

Had my high school years taken place today, I likely would never have been blessed with the close relationship I had with Christie's dad. She and I would have had mobile phones and I'd have been able to call her directly, thus short-circuiting any need for interaction with her parents.

If I'd had a mobile phone, I wouldn't have had to overcome near-crippling nerves to cross the playground and say a shy hello to Sarah James in Year 7; I could have just sent her a direct message or texted her a couple of emojis instead. I definitely wouldn't have had to call her home and introduce myself to her mum and dad, thus learning some of life's important conversational ropes.

Of course, every generation tends to look disapprovingly at the latest technology. First it was rock'n'roll on the radio that was going to rot kids' brains, then it was television and now it's 'screens', from smartphones to smart flat screens, tablets and even watches.

The explosion in phone technology, and the social media apps and gaming that clamour for space on phone screens, is barely a decade old, yet it's one of the things parents have asked me about most during presentations: 'How much of a role does social media play in our children's mental health?'

The truth is that it's way too early to say for sure, and, as I said earlier, the causes of mental illness are incredibly complex. But I would argue that, on the face of it, screens play a significant role in our mental health. Few people would disagree that as a society we have become addicted to our phones. We see this addiction reflected everywhere: parents take their kids to the park and disappear into their newsfeed; groups of schoolkids at bus stops might sit together but they're glued to the phones in their laps.

Some statistics: as of 2016, more than one million Australian teens between 14 and 17 – 91 per cent – had a mobile phone.[1] According to a 2017 survey run by the Royal Children's Hospital in Melbourne, parents estimate that their kids are spending on average 4.6 hours on a weekday and 4.5 hours on a weekend day using screen-based devices at home.[2] This is well in excess of the current Australian guidelines: up to one hour per day for children aged two to five years, and two hours per day for kids aged five to 17 years.[3]

Educators are all too aware of the problem. The New South Wales Department of Education cites a US study that found young people who spent more time on screens, including social media, were more likely to report mental health issues, including depression, than kids who engaged more with in-person social interaction, sports and homework.[4] Although the links between screen time and mental health are a matter of correlation rather than causation, teachers and governments are responding accordingly. The Victorian Government, for example, has adopted one of the world's toughest stances on mobile phone use in schools; from the start of 2020, students in primary and secondary schools will need to switch them off and store them in lockers while class is in session.[5]

It's not only adolescents who are increasingly immersing themselves in their smartphones and tablets. I've lost count of how many times parents have approached me after a presentation to confess to feeling guilty about looking at a little screen when they know they should be engaging with their kids.

The first thing we need to recognise is that none of this is our fault. We are being targeted by social media platforms that use manipulative techniques designed to keep us coming back to our screens.

Instagram, Facebook, Twitter, WhatsApp, Netflix, Snapchat, YouTube, etc. are fighting it out for the biggest slice of what's known as the 'attention economy'. The more time we spend on their sites, the more money they make, mostly through advertising. In mid-2019 there were 2.41 billion users of Facebook alone.[6] As marketplaces go, the attention economy is a monster and it feeds on our time.

According to Tristan Harris, a former design ethicist and product philosopher at Google, the best way to get people's attention is to know how their minds work. Once you do, says Harris, 'You can basically push their buttons and get them to not just come [to your platform] but to stay as long as possible.'[7]

And we thought we were the ones pushing the buttons!

Developers are locked in a race to come up with techniques designed solely to claim more territory in the attention landscape. These techniques are called 'persuasive technologies', which is really just jargon that explains the process of making these apps as psychologically addictive as possible. Thousands of highly intelligent developers and engineers spend their working days creating more ways to manipulate our minds.

Many apps, for example, build a 'variable schedule reward' into their platforms. It's exactly the same 'persuasive technology' used in poker machines. When players pull a handle on the pokies, they don't know for a few moments what 'reward' they're going to get; this seeking of different rewards becomes addictive. In the case of social media, you open Twitter, Instagram or Facebook and the app pauses for a second as it loads a 'variable reward', be it in the form of likes, new stories, a notification, or some other slippery digital slope for us to slide down.

Once the apps have us, they use a range of tricks to keep us there, like auto-loading videos, feeding us 'people you may know', and tracking our preferences then dangling them in front of us. And anyone who has ever tried to delete their Facebook account knows how time-consuming they have made that process.

Facebook has even figured out when we wake up. They know we're more likely to spend longer on their site if we're lying down, so when we wake up they drip-feed us alerts and notifications in a carefully researched shade of appealing red in order to keep us interested and in bed. They are playing with our minds to manipulate how we configure our bodies at the start of each day, and we don't even notice it's happening.

Tristan Harris, who quit Google and co-founded the Center for Humane Technology, says the deck is heavily stacked against consumers of social media. 'These companies often hide behind this notion that, "If you don't like it then stop using the product,"' he explains. 'But while they're saying that, they have teams of thousands of engineers whose job it is to deploy these techniques . . . to get people to spend as much time as possible there.'[8] That's like alcohol companies telling an alcoholic to simply stop drinking.

It's no wonder a 2017 Deloitte survey found Australians

checked their phones more than 35 times a day on average, an increase of around 17 per cent on just the year before.[9] Thirty-five per cent of us check our phone within five minutes of waking up in the morning, and 70 per cent use phones during mealtimes with family and friends.[10]

Needless to say, it's extremely hard to be mindful and mentally present when some of the world's biggest media corporations are trying to rip our time and attention from our hands. Smartphones are here to stay, and so is social media. And they're not the only threats; in 2018, the World Health Organization classified gaming addiction as a mental health disorder.[11] Our kids are copping it from everywhere.

That's the bad news. The good news is that we are not powerless, and the other side of this shiny technological coin has many benefits that can help enrich our lives. But we need to be careful. There are four simple strategies that I strongly recommend you try, so you can reclaim much of what the attention economy has taken from you:

1. DELETE FACEBOOK FROM OUR PHONES

On 2 July 2018, I dumped Facebook from my mobile and vowed only to look at it when I was using my laptop.

I haven't been on Facebook since, and it's not because I'm trying to avoid it – I'm just not as easy a target for Mark Zuckerberg's addiction engineers as I was when I had Facebook in my pocket.

The decision to delete the app was a life-changer. I didn't feel that I was any less connected to the people I wanted to connect with, and I realised I had spent most of my time on Facebook looking at garbage – stuff that, if someone asked me to check out in real life, I'd laugh at and walk away. I've often wondered how I'd react if I walked past a cafe, saw a friend and they said, 'Just in time! My coffee has arrived. Would you like to see how it looks from directly above?'

2. TURN OFF NOTIFICATIONS

There is no reason whatsoever to have notifications on our phones switched on. The only reason they exist is to suck us back into the app abyss. We don't need to know every single time someone has liked a photo, sent us a message, commented on a thread we're following or tagged us on Twitter. It's getting to the point where we don't really decide when we check our phones; our phones are deciding for us – more than 35 times a day!

3. REARRANGE OUR HOME SCREENS

The only apps we should have on our home screens are ones we're not addicted to. Once you clear all the addictive stuff off your home screen, you'll be amazed how few things you really 'need' on your phone. In my case I was left with just three apps: music, podcasts and Google Maps. That's it. Everything that has an addictive component I have placed in a separate file on the sixth screen across labelled 'Regret'.

4. LEAVE HOME WITHOUT OUR PHONES

When we disconnect from our phones we reconnect with life. Thanks largely to persuasive technology we've been conditioned to think we can't be without them. When we leave home these days we check that we have our keys, wallet, sunnies and . . . 'Where's my bloody phone?'

A few years back I started leaving mine at home at every opportunity. OK, often I need my phone for work, but do I need it if I'm going out to dinner? Going for a run? To the movies? Cricket training? Phones only serve to interrupt these moments and derail the joy of being present with the people we're with, even if that person is ourselves.

Not long after setting myself the rule about limiting my phone use, I caught up with a mate at a pub in Fitzroy.

It was a very quiet night at the pub as I sat at the bar and swapped stories with my mate. After a while he got up to go to the gents'. 'Back in a sec,' he said and disappeared. Suddenly I was one of only a few punters in the entire pub. Like Pavlov's dog I reached into my pocket to get my phone, and I actually felt annoyed that I'd left the thing at home.

I had nothing to do for the next minute or so. It was a strange feeling, like the world had stopped. 'How did we not look weird when we were sitting without anything to do, in the time before smartphones?' I pondered. That's when I noticed the barman just a few feet away, cleaning a pint glass.

'How's your night going?' I inquired. 'It's pretty quiet – you must love that?'

'No,' he said, 'I actually prefer it when it's busy.'

'Really?'

'Yeah,' he said. 'I'm just going through some difficult stuff at the moment and when it's really quiet I can't get it out of my head, but when it's busy I escape it for a bit.'

Suddenly I was in the midst of a serious moment with a fellow human being, and the world felt very full again. 'Oh,' I said, giving him my complete attention. 'Are you alright?'

'No, not really,' he replied. 'I'm just going through a breakup and it's pretty full-on at the moment.'

'I'm really sorry about that,' I said. 'I know exactly how that feels. It's awful.'

The barman and I were still talking about his situation five minutes after my mate returned.

'Anyway,' he said as a couple of customers appeared at the other end of the bar, 'I'll let you guys get back to it.'

'Take care of yourself, mate,' I said as he turned to serve the others. He flashed me a little thumbs up.

When I got home later, all I could think was, 'Thank God I left my phone here.' The barman clearly needed to reach out and make that connection in that moment; as soon as I opened my mouth to speak to him he grabbed the opportunity with both hands. If I'd had my phone with me, that conversation would never have happened. I'd have buried my head in the internet, and if the barman had wanted to talk about his emotional problems he'd have had to lean over and say, 'Excuse me, do you want to talk about my breakup for a minute?'

Increasingly, over the past ten years, more and more of us have been using social media to try to fulfil our basic psychological needs: the need to feel loved, to feel like we belong, to feel validated and achieve degrees of social status.

If we're hungry for love, we post a photo of ourselves and all people have to do is press a heart button to let us know they approve. If it's status we crave, we can simply add a 'status update' to show people we aced the job interview, took the holiday, skied down the mountain or welcomed the child. In return we hope our screens will bloom with little blue thumbs to feed our psychological hunger.

But it doesn't really nourish us. The flesh-and-blood thumbs up that the barman at the Union Club Hotel gave me meant more than a million likes on Facebook could. I imagine our talk that night meant much more to him than a sad-face emoji, too. This was an everyday illustration of the benefits of communication and social connection, something I am passionately advocating for day in, day out at The Resilience Project.

CHAPTER 9
KICK-OFF

On a stinking-hot Saturday afternoon in February 2015 I was padded up and ready to go in to bat for Melbourne University. We had a young new player in our side and his dad had come along to see his boy play, so I wandered over and introduced myself.

'If you've come to watch someone make a duck, your timing is perfect,' I said, extending my hand. (I'd come to terms with the fact that I was not a batsman a long time ago.) 'I'm Hugh. How are you going?'

'G'day, Hugh,' he said, shaking my hand. 'Brian Phelan.'

We had a nice chat about how well his son had been playing and how pleased I was to have him at MUCC. After a
while Brian asked what I did with myself outside of cricket.
I told him about The Resilience Project and his ears seemed
to prick up.

I explained how the organisation was based around
teaching the three principles of GEM, how you could practise them in everyday life, and what the benefits were. 'You
should come to my work and speak,' he said. 'We could really
use something like that.'

'Well, it's more something I've developed to help schoolchildren, Brian,' I pointed out. 'Where do you work anyway?'

'At the Melbourne Storm.'

As a Victorian boy I had grown up on AFL, but thanks
to the NRL's push into the state's sports market with the
mighty Melbourne Storm 17 years earlier, I was certainly
aware of a code called rugby league. I even knew the names
of the Storm's more famous players, like the superstars Billy
Slater and Cameron Smith. Everything else about the NRL,
however, was a bit of a mystery to me. I had never watched a
single game.

Despite my personal ignorance, the Storm had become
a pretty big deal in Melbourne. They'd notched up multiple
premiership wins and were backed by a world-class coaching

and administrative division. I figured Brian wanted me to share The Resilience Project with members of the club's back-end staff.

Before we could discuss it further, our second-last wicket fell and I had to go in to bat. 'Keep my seat warm – I'll be back in no time,' I said to my teammates. I shook hands with Brian, who said he'd call me on Monday. I pulled on my batting gloves, grabbed my bat and strode out the middle with a false bravado that only an experienced tail-ender is capable of. Sure enough, minutes later, I managed to miss a straight one. Afterwards I forgot all about the Melbourne Storm.

Two days later, Brian phoned as promised. 'When are you free to come and speak?' he asked.

'It kind of depends when your staff's available,' I replied. 'Who is it you want me to talk to exactly?'

'To the players!' he said, sounding surprised that I'd had to ask. 'I'm the player welfare manager.'

I was speechless for a moment. 'Ah, look mate,' I said, hesitating at the idea again, 'this is a presentation for school-kids. It's not really for footballers.'

'Have you done it for footballers before?' Brian asked.

'No.'

'Then how do you know it's not for footballers?'

'I don't know,' I said. 'I guess what I'm saying is it's not really my area of expertise.'

Brian was having none of it. 'You've played footy and cricket your entire life and you don't reckon sporting clubs are your area of expertise?'

'Oh well, maybe it's not that so much – it's just that I'm a schoolteacher.'

'And that's exactly why we need you. We want someone to come in and educate the boys with an important message,' he said. 'If it doesn't work it doesn't work, but let's at least give it a crack.'

A few days later I arrived early at the Storm's home ground at AAMI Park, just across the train tracks from the MCG. As hulking players filed into the meeting room I started to get nervous, which was a rare feeling for me before a talk. These men were the most powerfully built assortment of human beings I had seen gathered in the one spot. As I was only used to addressing schoolchildren, I felt completely out of place.

After the players had all taken a seat and Brian had finished his introduction, I managed to park my nerves and launch full throttle into my presentation. About five minutes in, I realised I had totally underestimated the power of the message; the looks on the players' faces were even more

engaged than any looks I'd seen in schools. They were leaning forward and listening intently to every word.

Fifteen minutes in, a player in the back row raised his
hand. 'Is this evidence-based?' he asked. 'Is this based on
scientifically researched material?'

In the previous four years of giving talks, I had never
been asked that question. Not by a teacher, not by a student, a psychologist, a doctor or any other professional
who'd heard the presentation at parents' nights. It took
a player from the NRL – a group of guys sometimes
maligned for being more brawn than brains – to raise it
with me.

'Yes, it is,' I assured the man in the back row. 'I'll send
you all the research later if you'd like.'

'Thanks,' he said. 'That'd be good. I want to have a look
at all the research. Knowing this stuff is evidence-based is
crucial.'

'Fair enough,' I said. 'I'll get it to you tomorrow.'

When my talk to the Storm players wrapped up, they
gave me a hearty round of applause. Several of the players
stopped and hugged me on the way out.

'That wasn't half bad,' Brian Phelan said with a wink
after all the players had left.

I had no choice but to agree with him. 'Tell me,' I said,

'who was that bloke in the back row who asked me about the research?'

Brian burst out laughing. 'That's Cooper Cronk!'

I laughed sheepishly and was forced to admit that I recognised the name but knew nothing about him. Today I am only too well aware who Cooper Cronk is: Australian representative, hero and architect of countless State of Origin series wins for Queensland, two-time winner of the coveted Dally M medal and one of the most humble and insightful people in elite sport I've ever met.

Brian called me again the following day. 'Hugh, the feeling in the office right now is electric,' he said. 'The boys are buzzing. They just loved the message. They want more. So, look, we need you back here next week and I've invited Paul Heptonstall, the head of player welfare at the NRL, to come and hear you too.'

Paul was sitting in the second-last row when I addressed the Storm players the following week. As soon as I finished he came straight over. 'We've got a conference coming up in two months and the wellbeing staff from every club in the league are going to be there,' he explained. 'I need you to speak to them.'

After I finished chatting with Paul, Brian came over and informed me that the club leaders Cameron Smith, Cooper

Cronk and Billy Slater had demanded that the program be rolled out across the entire club. Cameron Smith was particularly passionate about the whole club experiencing the program.

'We'd like you to give your talk to the under-20s players, the under-18s and the under-16s,' Cameron said. 'We'd like you to speak to all the players' partners, to all the staff at the club and the sponsors, too.'

Over the next six months I visited AAMI Park countless times to give the talk about gratitude, empathy and mindfulness because Cameron, Billy and Cooper had pretty much said, 'You're doing it.' All of them championed The Resilience Project and wove GEM not only into the fabric of their club but into their personal lives, too.

I was thrilled the day Billy Slater sent me a message asking whether he could get a couple more resilience journals so his family could get stuck in as well. The next day, as I was driving to Billy's house to drop them in the letterbox, I saw Billy and his wife, Nicole, having a coffee out the front of their local cafe. I pulled up and joined them, and they told me how excited they were for their kids to start thinking about resilience and GEM.

Their daughter has used the journals in order to practise gratitude. Every night, before she goes to bed, she reflects on what went well during her day to settle her mind. Nicole says she's noticed a massive difference: their daughter looks forward to spending time with her family and going to school more.

The Slaters also make a habit of discussing how their days went around the dinner table every night. They always try to be as positive and grateful as they can, focusing on the amazing opportunities in their and their kids' lives.

Billy was a big believer in practising empathy, too. He wound up injured not long after I started working with the Storm, and on a chilly afternoon in Sydney, while his teammates were warming up to play against the Roosters, he decided to go for a run to stay as sharp as possible since he wasn't playing. Halfway through the run, Billy came across some homeless people in a park. Moved by the sight of them, and with the concept of empathy fresh in his mind, he headed over to the supermarket and bought lunch for them.

'I know it must have improved their day a little,' he told me later, 'but I wasn't expecting that *I'd* be buzzing about it weeks later.'

At the NRL conference in Sydney I discovered I still had a lot to learn about rugby league. As I was getting ready to address player welfare staff I was introduced to some absolute giants of the game, and I was ashamed to admit I didn't have a clue who they were. I was embarrassed at the sheer ignorance because I love sport; I know every AFL and VFL footballer who's ever played the game, and I know every cricketer who has ever played for Australia or their state. It just goes to show how polarised Australians can be when it comes to football. For me, at least, that was about to change.

After I addressed the NRL conference, each and every one of the 16 clubs in the competition booked me to speak to their players and staff about resilience. In fact, Paul made my visits to the clubs an NRL-mandated program. Over the next seven months I spent a week with each club, and I did six presentations within that week.

Like a lot of people who hear my talk, the NRL guys seemed to be captivated by the stories about Stanzin and his appreciation for everything he considered good in his life. They loved the idea of being so grateful to have basic comforts that one might point at one of them and say, 'Dis!'

I asked some of the Storm players if they'd like to do the 'Dis Challenge', an activity that had proven to be popular in schools. 'It's pretty simple,' I said. 'Over the next twenty-four hours, whenever you see something you're very grateful for – I don't care where you are or who you are with – I'd like you to stop, point to it and say "Dis!"' They were keen to give it a go.

As the players were filing out of the room afterwards, one of them hung back and approached me as I was packing up my laptop. He asked if he could show me something. When I said yes, he stood there and eyeballed me for a second or two, then pulled up his football jumper to reveal the most ridiculous sixpack I have ever seen. 'Dis!' he said, jabbing a finger at his abdominals, before walking out of the room with a smile.

By the time I was halfway through the NRL program I felt I'd found my feet and understood the culture of rugby league a little better. I've never been one to swagger, but I had certainly gained some confidence. I was on my way to talk to the Penrith Panthers one morning when I received a call from their player welfare manager.

'Just a tip, Hugh – you'll want to get to the ground half an hour early and make sure you're ready to start when the players arrive,' she advised me.

'I'm always half an hour early, but today I'll make sure I'm there forty-five minutes beforehand,' I promised.

'Yeah, probably a good idea,' she said. 'Trust me – you

want to be fully set up and ready to roll as soon as the guys'
bums hit the seats.'

I assured her I would. Clearly the Panthers were under
a bit of time pressure.

I arrived at their home ground in Western Sydney with
plenty of time to spare. The conference room was on the
fourth floor of the grandstand, so I headed over to the lift
with my gear. Just as I stepped inside two players appeared
around the corner and yelled out, 'Hey mate, hold the lift
will you?'

After they climbed in with me, another two players piled
in, then another two. Suddenly I was squashed against the
back of the lift by six of the biggest men I have ever seen in
my life. As the doors of the lift finally slid shut one of the
players asked, 'How long is this bloke supposed to be talking
for anyway?'

'Apparently it's an hour,' a teammate answered.

'Oh, for fuck's sake!' the first player groaned. 'An hour?
You've gotta be kidding.'

'That's what they said,' his mate replied.

'What's he talking about?' the first guy said.

'Resilience, I think,' came the reply.

'Oh you are fucking kidding me,' he said, sounding shattered. 'Don't worry about it, boys – if this bloke goes for

a minute over an hour, I'll just get up and punch him in the face.'

The players laughed while a little part of me died inside. 'Ah, guys,' I said as quietly and politely as I could, 'I'm actually in the lift with you. I'm the one doing the talk.'

There was a momentary silence as the players revelled in the awkwardness, trying not to laugh. The first player didn't even bother to turn around, however; he just raised a clenched fist and growled, 'Don't go for more than an hour, champion!'

Later on I learned this guy's name was Jamie Soward, premiership winner and State of Origin player. It was an absolute pleasure to meet him after the session . . . which happened to last well over an hour. He was very apologetic, and generous with his praise for the talk.

I was constantly blown away by the NRL players. It's no secret that some of them struggled with problems off the field, and it seemed like every season was marred by some kind of personal scandal. In some pockets of the press and among certain members of the public, rugby league footballers were considered boorish and spoilt. In my experience – and I met just about all of them and developed close relationships with many – I found them to be the opposite.

When I finish a talk for teachers or in the corporate world, I'm accustomed to the odd person coming to the front to say thank you, but most will head for the door – which is fine, of course, as I don't expect a personal thanks from every audience member. NRL players, however, have been the most well-mannered, kind and loving group I've presented to. It's common for them to line up afterwards to give me a hug or an extremely cool handshake I can't keep up with.

One Roosters player I came to know was front-rower Martin Kennedy. My first day at the club Martin came in at the last minute and sat right up the back of the room. As soon as I started talking he pulled his hoodie over his face, put his head down and didn't look up for the next hour and a half. 'This guy,' I thought to myself, 'is absolutely hating this.'

Afterwards, the rest of the players came over to thank me for the talk, and to grab one of the wellbeing journals that were on offer. Martin walked straight past me, but just as he neared the door he turned and looked directly at me. I didn't know what his name was, let alone what was going on with him, and the next second he was gone.

A year later I was giving a public talk in front of 600 people at the Wesley Mission's Conference Centre in the Sydney CBD. As I was walking onto the stage I took a quick look at the people in the front rows and was surprised to see the player from the Sydney Roosters, who was sitting alongside an older woman.

He pulled his cap over his eyes and put his head down a number of times during the talk. 'What is he doing back here if he hates it so much?' I wondered. When the talk finished a few people came up to speak to me, and when they'd thinned out I felt a large hand on my shoulder.

'Hey mate, you don't know who I am. My name's Martin Kennedy and I was in the talk you did at the Roosters last year,' he said.

'Hi Martin. Actually, I do remember you.'

'Anyway, this is my mum,' he continued, gesturing to the woman standing next to him. 'I wanted to bring her along tonight . . .'

Before he could get another word out, he started to sob. His mum hugged him, tears welling in her eyes too. Finally Martin pulled himself together enough to continue with what he'd wanted to tell me: 'You're the only reason I'm alive,' he said.

I was floored. Looking at his mum, I became quite teary myself. Martin continued: 'I made a decision the day before your talk that I was going to go down to Mum and Dad's beach house and I was going to end it all.' I noticed Martin's mum was holding his arm tight. 'But the next day I heard you speak and I'm still here, mate.' He tapped a fist gently against his broad chest, as if to suggest his beating heart was evidence of a battle that he was proud to have won. 'I'm still breathing, brother –' he reached out to hug me – 'and it's because of your talk.'

By the time I finished working with all grades of every club in the NRL, I had received emails from four more players who said the Resilience Project talk is the only thing that had kept them from committing suicide.

That's five reasons I will never stop pushing The Resilience Project's message, as long as I live.

CHAPTER 10

PENNY

When I first met my wife, she was 13 and I was 20. And she was on a date with my little brother. I know what you're thinking! Bear with me.

Josh came home from school one day in Year 8 feeling pretty pleased with himself. There was a new girl in the year below him and she was the talk of the school. He'd asked her if he could take her out on a date with him. She'd said yes.

'That's amazing!' I was ecstatic for him; he'd been talking about her nonstop for the past week, so this was big news. 'So what's the plan? Where are you going to take her?'

'I have no idea . . .' he said, a grin still plastered across his face.

We both knew where this was heading. As a 14-year-old schoolboy Josh wasn't exactly rolling in money, and at times like these it was a major plus to have a big brother who controlled the candy bar at Balwyn Cinema.

When Saturday night rolled around I was behind the counter when Josh walked in with his date, Miss Penelope Moodie.

Still reeling from the infamous 'Cheezels in the storeroom' incident (see Chapter 2), I was trying ever so hard to be the consummate employee. But as soon as I saw Josh stumble into the cinema foyer, a nervous wreck, I knew exactly where my loyalties lay. Josh has always been my best friend, and I've seen it as my duty to make his life as smooth as possible. On this occasion, that meant free entry to the cinema and a free run of the candy bar. He and Penny loaded up on choc-tops and lollies, and trotted into Cinema 2 to watch the 8 pm screening of *Shrek*.

At that time, things were pretty grim at home. Georgia was close to her lowest weight so it was nice to see Josh out of the house, and looking so happy and excited. Penny seemed like a lovely kid, too.

No sooner had they taken their seats than seven of my mates bowled through the front door of the cinema.

'What movies are you showing, Hugh?' they wanted to know.

Worried that they'd ruin Josh's date, I subtly tried to steer them away from *Shrek*, which a couple of the boys were already lobbying for. 'I've heard good things about *Tomb Raider*...'

'What about *Shrek*?' one of the boys cut in. 'It has the guy from *Wayne's World*, whatsizname, Mike Myers.'

'Nah, you don't wanna see *Shrek*!' I said, but they knew me too well. They zeroed in.

'Why don't you want us to see *Shrek*?'

'Nothing,' I said. 'It's just . . . you wouldn't like it. Trust me. No *Shrek*. Not *Shrek*.'

'We're definitely seeing *Shrek* now, mate. Who's in there?'

'Fuck, alright,' I said. 'It's Josh, OK? He's brought a date and there's hardly anyone else in there with them, so why don't we just leave them alone?'

Not a chance.

'We'll have seven tickets for *Shrek* please, Hugh.'

The cinema was all but empty, and they could have chosen to sit anywhere they wanted. Of course they parked themselves directly behind the young lovebirds. Josh started to sweat profusely, but about halfway through the movie he worked up the nerve to put his hand on Penny's leg.

He reckons his palm was so sweaty it stuck to her like glue. My evil mates relayed the information along the line in Chinese whispers:

'Hand on leg.'

'Hand on leg.'

'Hand on leg.'

'We've got a hand on leg . . .'

Poor Josh and Penny. Their teenage crush eventually faded, and Josh came to see the funny side of that date night. I know this for a fact because, as my best man, he told the story at Penny's and my wedding 18 years later.

When it came time for *my* first date with Penny in 2015, I left absolutely nothing to chance.

Years earlier we'd ended up friends on Facebook and I'd bumped into her a few times through people we both knew. I thought adult Penny was incredibly beautiful, the kind of beautiful that gets inside your head and steals your attention away from what you're doing. She had a breathtaking smile.

After we exchanged a series of awkward Facebook messages over the course of six months, I summoned up the courage to ask Penny for a coffee catch-up under the pretence of having a chat about work-related matters; she was working in public health at the time. We met in a really cool cafe tucked away near Melbourne University. I didn't know much about Penny but I did know she was highly intelligent, so somehow I thought catching up near the uni would give me an impression of intelligence by proxy.

We sat side-by-side at the end of a long communal table. Five minutes into our 'work chat', even though I didn't know her own relationship status, I just knew she was the one. A few days later, I worked up the courage to ask her out – on a proper date this time. We agreed to catch up for a drink that coming Sunday.

I wanted everything to be perfect so I carried out detailed reconnaissance on eight different venues as I searched Melbourne for the perfect place to take her. I obsessed over the criteria – I wanted the place to be cool but not too loud, cosy but not cramped, and I wanted us to sit next to each other on high stools instead of looking directly at each other across a table. I had it all figured out.

After hours spent checking out spots, I ultimately decided on a well-hidden cocktail bar in Fitzroy. There I found the perfect nook to take Penny: an intimate corner of the bar that had two high stools and a little bench jutting off the wall. I asked the manager if I could reserve the slice of first-date heaven but was told they didn't take bookings. 'If you want to sit there,' the manager said, 'just get here early.'

I'd arranged to meet Penny at 8 pm so I arrived half an hour early and staked my claim to the magical stools in the corner. Penny walked in on the stroke of eight. 'Hi!' she said as we gave each other a little hug. 'How are you? Wow, this is a strange place to sit. Why did they make you sit here?'

'Oh, yeah, it's totally weird, isn't it?' I said, cringing inside. 'The barman said I should sit here.'

'It's an awkward place to sit. Let's find somewhere else.'

'Lead the way!'

We ended up perched opposite each other at a little table. We drank cocktails until 2 am and didn't take a breath from conversation. I could have listened to Penny talk all night. It took me less than eight hours to fall completely in love with her. Within a month she became my best friend, and I knew I wanted to spend the rest of my life with her.

For someone who made me feel on top of the world, Penny made me feel very calm, too. For once I was totally and utterly comfortable being myself, saying exactly what I thought and not trying too hard – like that guy who did hours of detailed research into where to sit in a bar.

■

We'd only been together a few weeks when I started to sus-pect Penny might suffer from anxiety. I noticed she was quite on edge in really special moments. The day after she first stayed over at my place I was absolutely over the moon, but Penny's mood and body language seemed to belong to someone who'd regretted the previous night. At first I was shattered: there I was, with a person I was in love with, and all I could think was, 'She doesn't want to be here.'

Still, we went out for a coffee and after she headed back to her place I thought, 'I'll probably never see her again.' I didn't hear from Penny that day, which meant I hardly slept that night. The next morning I sent her a message: 'Hey!'

She wrote back immediately: 'I just heard about this cinema opening in St Kilda. What time do you want to meet? We'll go there tonight. Can't wait to see you, I've been thinking about you heaps today.'

Oh, the relief. The next morning, however, Penny seemed anxious again. She started rhythmically tapping with her hand, and couldn't seem to stop or stay still. A few weeks later Penny told me she suffered from anxiety and obses-sive-compulsive disorder (OCD). She took antidepressant medication every day.

My first reaction was sadness for her. I was having all these amazing feelings, and although Penny said she had fallen in love too, it seemed clear she wasn't able to totally immerse herself in those feelings. Although the antidepressants helped prevent her from bottoming out emotionally, they also kept her from experiencing life's highs.

Penny was eight when she started showing signs of OCD. Today she gets really upset when people make flippant remarks about the condition and misrepresent what it does to people. You often hear people say things like, 'I'm so OCD about cleaning my room' or 'My husband is OCD about the grocery shopping.' Those are not examples of OCD – they're examples of being fastidiously tidy or having a system when you do the shopping.

Obsessive-compulsive disorder is a whole other kettle of awful. As Penny puts it: 'OCD is convincing yourself you have AIDS at the age of eight and worrying yourself sick about it for the next four years. It's getting your camera out every time you have to turn off a switch because you won't ever trust that you did it in the first place without solid evidence. It is emotionally and physically exhausting.'

These days she sees an incredible psychologist who hosts group sessions with five other women around the same age as Penny so they can share their experiences with OCD and support one another. These women's stories are both heartbreaking and inspiring.

Penny is up against a sabotaging inner voice. When we got engaged she couldn't stop thinking, 'You actually don't want to marry Hugh. You're not in love with him at all.' Even though Penny knew she was in love and that she did want to get married to me, she had to face down this destructive voice.

Every toilet seat in every house Penny and I have ever lived in has been broken due to a lingering obsession with sitting a certain way to avoid germs. Sometimes she can get stuck in the shower, too, staring endlessly at the floor, ruminating about all the big decisions she's made in her life and wondering if she's made the wrong one every time. She finds it hard to enjoy the good things that happen because this inner voice constantly seeks to find the negative in any situation.

Another thing I love about Penny is how hard she fights back against it all.

While Penny has always been an empathetic person, practising gratitude didn't come quite as naturally to her; the negative thoughts associated with her mental illness would usually crowd out the optimism trying to get through. But ever since she started her practice – listing three things that have gone well for her during the day, every night before bed – she has noticed a gradual change. The practice has allowed Penny to catastrophise less, and has tempered the emotional impact of negative thought cycles.

Mindfulness might be a bit of a buzzword these days, but it is far from a new fad; people have been meditating in many cultures for millennia. The neuroscientific research into its related benefits, which started appearing around 40 years ago, is fascinating.

There are many ways to meditate; from mindfulness practice to mantra meditation, there are hundreds of techniques out there. In recent years, Penny has chosen to immerse herself in Vipassana meditation – an intense, committed approach, derived from Buddhist practice, that requires participants to attend a silent retreat for ten days.

The first time Penny went on a retreat, her anxiety had been at its worst. At the retreat she'd wake each day at 4 am and meditate until 6.30, before having a simple breakfast. She'd then meditate from 7.30 to 11, and then – after lunch and an hour's break – she'd meditate for another four hours in the afternoon. 'Dinner', which consisted of a piece of fruit and a cup of tea, was at 5 pm, followed by another two hours of meditation before she was in bed by 9.

Penny said the experience led to intense mental and

physical pain, as deeply buried emotions, fears and regrets floated up to the conscious level. 'Everything I'd been suppressing, everything I'd been holding back, everything I'd been masking, all my insecurities, all the things I don't like about myself – they came out during the ten days,' she explained to me later.

'You sit cross-legged on a hard floor and it hurts, but by trying to observe the pain rather than react to it, it tends to dissipate. The same goes for emotional pain.'

By day seven or eight, however, Penny said she'd never felt emotional or physical suffering like it. 'I could actually see my car from where I had lunch each day,' she recalled. 'That was the most painful part – I could just get in the car and go if I wanted to. I didn't have to stay.

'But on day nine and ten, when all the stuff I was insecure about came out – the painful memories, things I'd pushed to the side and hoped would never resurface – they all arose in a really peaceful way. I was able to accept that these things were part of who I am. I was grateful I'd been through those experiences and grateful they were part of my personality.'

For someone who had struggled with severe anxiety and OCD, Penny said meditation was one of the most powerful things she's ever done to help put her in a better place.

I was so glad Penny did Vipassana meditation. She

definitely needed it, partly in order to be able to put up with me.

Past girlfriends hadn't always embraced my love of sport. Some outwardly hated it when I was off on my own and immersed in cricket. One of the countless things I found attractive about Penny was her total support for the things I already loved in life. As I juggled The Resilience Project and my cricket commitments, she demonstrated a huge amount of selflessness in forfeiting summer weekends with me, along with two nights for training every week. 'I love that you play cricket,' she'd say. 'It's great to have passion.'

It was the same when it came to work. If I had to go interstate for a week, or talk to schoolchildren throughout regional Victoria, she'd help get me out the door on time: 'Go and do what you've gotta do,' she'd say with a loving kiss. 'I'll see you when you get home.'

In 2017, Penny and I welcomed a beautiful little boy, Benji. The day of his birth was the single greatest moment of my life. Finally – for the first time since I started playing grade cricket at the age of 15 – I thought it might be time to retire from club cricket. I hung on at MUCC as coach for another year or so but in the end I gave that away too.

Spending every weekend plus Tuesday and Thursday nights away from Penny and Benji wouldn't have been fair, nor was it remotely appealing to me anymore.

When I told Penny I was considering a return to competitive sport just a few months later, I don't think she was disappointed; she just wasn't expecting it. Instead of cricket, though, I had somehow got my heart set on athletics – a good 20 years after I had last competed as a schoolboy.

After retiring from cricket, I had quickly found I missed the exercise that went with it. I had always trained with a goal in mind as opposed to for the hell of it, and in 2017 I fixated on the goal of returning to the track. I was a little nervous about breaking the news to Penny, however, because I recognised the idea was a bit on the eccentric side. True to form, her response was direct.

'That is such a strange thing for someone of your age to do,' she said.

'Yeah, I know,' I said, nodding. 'A thirty-seven-year-old wannabe sprinter.'

But she was totally supportive. 'Well,' she said, 'I look forward to coming to watch you.'

What a gal.

I never went so far as to get a coach, but I looked up

training programs online and designed a schedule that involved four track sessions and three gym sessions a week.

At the first race meeting I attended, I assumed I'd be running in a Masters division with other blokes my age. In Round One, all entrants had to nominate what time we thought we might run the 400 metres in so they could arrange us into graded heats.

When my turn came I sauntered out onto the track, shook out my arms and legs, and bounced on my toes a couple of times like you see the big guns do before an Olympic event. I got down on my haunches, put my feet in the starting blocks and only then did I take a look at my competition. On my right were two silver-haired men in their sixties and to my left were two boys aged ten or 11.

'On your marks,' the official said.

I looked over at Penny, who was standing 20 metres away with Benji snuggled against her chest. She was smiling, shaking her head and clearly mouthing the words, 'What the fuck are you doing?'

'Get set . . .'

Bang. The starter's gun brought me back to the moment, but in those 400 metres all I could think about was Penny's quizzical grin. 'What the fuck *am* I doing? I'm running against sixty-year-old men and a couple of primary school kids?'

There was no audible applause when I came first by a country mile. I imagine a few people watching wondered if there was something wrong with me. But when I was told what time I had run, I was pretty pleased: one minute and one second.

'Oh wow,' I told Penny. 'That's not terrible.'

When we got in the car to go home Penny said, 'So I guess that's the last time you'll ever do that?'

'Actually,' I said, 'I think I want to do this properly.'

'You're kidding me,' she said, turning her body in the passenger seat to face me. 'You're going to race against little boys and old men?'

'Well, hopefully I'll get better,' I said.

'Oh my God,' she said, returning her gaze to the road ahead. 'It's a good thing I love you.'

I trained hard and competed at lots of events over the next ten months, and my times kept coming down. My ultimate goal was to do well in what I considered the marquee event of the season: the Victorian Masters Track & Field Championships. That's where I could expect to run against the best guys my age and see how I really stacked up as an athlete.

When my day of reckoning finally came, Penny and Benji were at Box Hill Athletic Club to see me test myself against some worthy opponents. I eyeballed quite a few blokes who looked about my age as we warmed up, did stretches and fussed over our running spikes. I felt a surge of competitive adrenaline and a sense of achievement that I'd arrived at my end goal. I'd worked hard and I knew I had just as much chance as anyone of winning a medal.

When the men's 35-to-40 years 400 metres was announced, it turned out there were no heats – just one race, the final. Mine was the first name called out over the PA: 'In lane one, Hugh van Cuylenburg, Melbourne University Athletics Club.'

Mine was also the last name called out. A bemused official beckoned me over to her. 'Um, you're the only person in your age group,' she said. 'Let me see what we can do about it.' Rather than force me to go the Monty Python route and run a race by myself, the marshals kindly bumped me up an age group to run with the 40-to-45-years blokes.

Even though I wasn't technically racing against them, only alongside them, I came in a respectable second place, with a time of 53 seconds. Afterwards, I got to climb to the top of the winners' podium all by myself. As Victoria's fastest – and only – 'Master' in his late thirties, I was presented with a gold medal.

I looked over to Penny for her approval. She had her phone out, to take photos of me on the podium, I assumed.

After the ceremony, euphoric from my sprinting triumph and poised to launch into a detailed analysis of the race, I asked Penny if she'd taken a good shot.

'What, of you?' She sounded surprised. 'No, sorry, but I got this great one of a ninety-five-year-old man in a one-piece sprinting outfit.' She showed me. 'Check it out – what a legend! Please tell me you'll wear something like that next season.'

Over the years I came to understand that being physically healthy is an important component of maintaining better mental health. Exercise plays a big role in Penny's management of her anxiety and OCD, too. After she exercises in the morning she's a different person, and copes so much better with the pressure of the day-to-day.

Falling in love with Penny coincided with The Resilience Project's expansion into working with elite sportspeople via the NRL. On average I was away from home four nights a week as I travelled around Australia speaking to rugby league clubs and maintaining my work teaching GEM in schools.

If I hadn't had Penny's support and her belief in The Resilience Project, I'm not sure I'd have been able to keep it up. Over the first three years, from 2011 to 2013, I'd become physically and mentally drained as I tried to meet the growing demand for GEM in schools and beyond. As soon as I had Penny in my life, though, I felt once again that I wanted to keep doing it forever.

The arrival of Benji in 2017 added another layer of love and purpose to our lives. It also happened to coincide with another huge expansion in The Resilience Project's reach and workload. Another football code expressed interest in bringing the principles of GEM into the game. This time I knew all of the players' names by heart.

CHAPTER 11
PLAY ON

The Resilience Project started to attract a bit of publicity during the time I worked with the NRL, so it wasn't a great surprise when some clubs in the AFL sought our help in player welfare. It was obvious from the start that some stars of the game faced similar challenges to their counterparts in rugby league.

Many of the nation's most talked-about young men struggled with an alarming amount of pressure. Elite sport goes hand in hand with media scrutiny, a loss of privacy, the weight of expectation and sometimes brutal public criticism.

Players must cope with all of that on top of the daily grind that results in one in five of all Australian adults battling some kind of mental health problem each year.

One of the first teams I spoke to was the Richmond Football Club. My initial contact with the club was actually with one of their star players, David Astbury, who told me, 'I've heard about your work, mate. We need this stuff at our club. I'd love for you to come and speak to us.'

A few days before I was due to present at Richmond, I caught up with David for a coffee.

'I want to hear everything you're going to say and I want to hear it before the rest of the team hears it,' he said.

'What a competitive young man,' I thought to myself. Little did I know he just wanted me to position the talk in a way that would maximise impact with his group of peers.

I outlined what The Resilience Project was all about and how we operated.

'I love it,' David said when I'd finished. 'I love anything to do with improving wellbeing and I value what you've said, but I've got some feedback for you.'

'I'd really like to hear it,' I said.

'We're footballers,' he said bluntly.

'And?'

'Are you just going to tell us this stuff and we have to walk away and magically bring these concepts into our lives?'

'That's the idea.'

'Mate, you've got to give us something tangible to do. We're footballers – give us something to practise and I'll tell you right now we'll commit to it better than most people because that's what we do, we practise in order to get the results.'

The next day I arrived at Punt Road Oval, Richmond's spiritual home, armed with copies of our 21-day wellbeing journal. (See page 259 at the back of the book for some sample exercises from the journals.) After I delivered the talk, the players filed past and took a journal each from the pile. When star midfielder Dustin Martin walked past he looked at me then looked at the stack of journals, grabbed ten and left.

Exactly 210 days later, I was having breakfast with Penny when my phone hummed with an incoming text message. I didn't recognise the number.

'Hi mate,' it read. 'Finished the journals. Can you please send me some more?'

Stumped, I wrote back, 'I'm so sorry, but who is this?'

'It's Dusty.'

'Sorry, Dusty who?'

'It's Dustin Martin, Richmond Football Club.'

I dropped my phone and said to Penny, 'It's Dustin Martin from the Richmond Football Club!', then continued the conversation by text.

'I took a stack of your journals,' he wrote.

'Yeah, I noticed that.'

'Well, I haven't missed a day. I've done two hundred and ten in a row. Every day I write down all the things that go well for me, the things I'm so grateful for. It's unbelievable how much it has changed me but I don't want to miss another day. Can you please send me some more journals? Preferably before tomorrow.'

'We actually have a six-month journal,' I told him. 'Would you like one of those?'

'Geez,' he wrote, 'it would have been good to know that two hundred and ten days ago!'

In early 2019, Dustin and I spoke at a conference together. He told the audience he was up to 1086 consecutive days of doing the Resilience Project journal, which takes about ten minutes each night.

'It takes ten minutes every night,' he said. 'The thing is, you can't just walk away after hearing about GEM and think, "That's nice. I'm going to be more grateful and more empathetic and more mindful." If you want to be good at something you have to practise it. I understand that because

I'm an elite sportsperson. I know how to train, how to practise these things.'

Dustin's teammate David Astbury had been right. Knowing about wellbeing is one thing; practising it and getting better at it is another thing altogether.

Dustin would be the first to admit he struggled with some off-field issues early in his career, but today he seems a different man. During the 2019 pre-season, I was having lunch with Dustin and his best mate, the inspirational Richmond captain Trent Cotchin. Trent was in the midst of telling us a great story and Dustin and I were both leaning in, listening intently. Just as Trent was getting to the pointy end of the story, a guy in a suit came straight over and crashed into our conversation without so much as an 'excuse me'.

'Here's the "before" picture,' said the suit, holding up his phone and showing us an old selfie he'd taken with Dustin. 'That was ten years ago. Now let's do the "after" picture.'

Trent and I shot the guy a look that said, 'Are you serious?'

The suit threw an arm around Dustin and took the photo without properly asking, then disappeared without a thank you.

'Geez, that must be bloody annoying,' I said to Dustin.

'Oh, it's not ideal, mate,' Dustin agreed. 'But it's not the end of the world either. I'm sure there are people out there dealing with far greater problems.'

I'm always blown away by Dustin's insight, and his willingness to do work in order to grow into the best version of himself. I wouldn't dream of claiming that practising GEM principles is the reason for Dustin's stellar run in 2017 – in which he won the Norm Smith and Brownlow medals along with the Coaches Association Player of the Year when Richmond won the premiership – but I do know it has helped him to feel happier, more balanced and well rounded.

Sharing the stories of Stanzin and Georgia can be a very emotional experience for me. Even now, after years of telling complete strangers the intimate details of my family's suffering, I can sometimes find myself getting teary. I've also developed a sixth sense for how certain audiences might react to aspects of the talk. Whenever I sense people are feeling a little fragile, I pull back on the emotion so as not to upset them. One of the most moving occasions involved an absolute legend of the AFL, St Kilda's beloved captain Nick Riewoldt.

On the day I was due to talk to the Saints, Nick approached the club's player welfare manager, who was sitting beside me as the players filed in.

'I don't have to hang around for this, do I?' Nick asked.

'Yeah,' the welfare manager said. 'Hugh's going to talk about resilience. I think you'll get a lot out of it.'

Nick politely introduced himself to me, shook my hand and welcomed me to the club. Then he turned back to the welfare manager. 'No offence, but I really don't need to be here for this,' he said. 'I've sat through so many presentations on this stuff. I think my time would be much better spent on the physio table.' But the welfare manager insisted Nick stay.

The exchange left me feeling a bit flat. I'd always put Nick Riewoldt on a pedestal – not only as a power forward but also as an ambassador for the game, a beacon for good sportsmanship and a shining example of a dedicated club man. I was so excited about this session with the Saints, and it was mostly because of him. Knowing that he didn't want to be there left me feeling pretty shattered.

In the end Nick begrudgingly took a seat in the very back row, as players often do if they feel they're not going to be engaged.

I was only two minutes in when I perused the room to see how the players were holding up as I spoke to them about Georgia's seemingly unstoppable slide towards death. I was surprised to see Nick Riewoldt looking directly at me, with tears streaming down his face. When our eyes met, he pulled his cap over his face and lowered his head. The next time I looked at Nick, his head was rested on a teammate's shoulder.

Nick had lost his sister, Madeleine, to a rare bone marrow disorder a couple of years earlier. The story of what happened to my sister was close to his heart.

When the talk moved on from Georgia, Nick's body language shifted; he leaned forward, spun his cap around backwards, lifted his head and started nodding in agreement throughout the remainder of the session. For the next hour the St Kilda captain was fully engaged. When I finished the presentation, he made a beeline for me and was the first player to thank me. He gave me a huge hug and said, 'You have no idea how much I needed to hear that.'

The experience reminded me that we're all working our way through our own issues, and that no one is immune to trauma. One of the main lessons I've taken from my work with The Resilience Project is that when you're willing to make yourself vulnerable and open up about your hardships, you give others around you the permission to open up about their own struggles. It's a message of trust, extended from one person to another.

■

At Collingwood Football Club, the story of Stanzin made a huge impact on the players. One day I noticed captain Scott Pendlebury had posted a photo on social media with the caption, 'Dis moment #gratitude.'

'What's all that about?' I asked when I next saw him.

'That little boy you told us about,' Scott replied. 'I really loved that story. I'm living out my dream with footy, but we can all get stuck thinking about the negatives in life. His story has really helped me to see the positives. And by the way, next time you're watching, pay close attention to Adam Treloar. If you can get a photo of his wrist, just have a close look.'

'How come?' I asked.

'Just have a look.'

It turned out that after the Resilience Project talk, star midfielder Treloar – who has since revealed he's battled severe anxiety during his career – had started writing 'DIS' in large black letters on his wrist strapping in preparation for every game. Before he ran out, he would tap his wrist and say to himself, 'Adam, you are blessed.'

When I saw him next, I asked him what made him feel blessed – was it being grateful to play AFL in front of all those people?

'I live in Australia,' Adam said. 'We get food, we get

water, we get shelter. I remind myself of that whenever I get stressed. "Dis" means this life in this country, every day.'

In the case of Collingwood coach Nathan Buckley, a constant practice of cultivating empathy has had a massive impact on how he approaches life. At my first session with the Magpies in 2015, it was clear Nathan was under enormous pressure because the team wasn't winning. I'm not a motivational speaker in the mould of Beefy but I do remember saying to Nathan and the players, 'Winning or losing is not going to make you feel happy or sad. Doing things for other people – that's what makes you feel good.'

Maybe it's his background as a footballer, but Nathan knows you don't improve if you don't practise, and he has since made a virtue out of being kind to others. He won't give me permission to mention some of the random acts of kindness – sometimes extreme kindness – he's been responsible for over the past few years because he doesn't want to trade on it or have it seem like a PR exercise. 'It's personal,' he has said. 'It's between me and the people I interact with in my life.'

I can share one story, though, because I was there to see it so it is also my tale to tell. I was among the 10,000 people who turned up to watch Collingwood's grand final training session at the Holden Centre three days before the 2018 decider. There wasn't much room where I was standing and I was positioned right alongside a man in his fifties who was in a wheelchair. He was wrapped in a Collingwood scarf and beanie, but he was painfully frail; he needed oxygen to breathe and he was clearly terminally ill.

Training was in full swing when Nathan drifted over to near where we were positioned. He turned around and started waving his arms. I waved back. 'G'day Bucks,' I called out.

He jogged over a little closer. 'Not you!' he said. 'The guy next to you.'

Nathan was worried the man in the wheelchair couldn't see training properly from his seated position. Before I knew it, Nathan had asked me to help bring the man out onto the field so he could see the Magpies go through their motions.

When I next saw them, Nathan was chatting away to the bloke. He revealed he'd been a diehard Pies supporter for half a century, and his dream was to see one more Collingwood premiership.

'I can't promise you that,' Nathan told him, 'but I can promise you you'll have a great day today.'

Nathan made sure the man was front and centre during the entire training session. Afterwards all the players introduced themselves to him and posed for photographs. I will never forget the look on that man's face as he was showered with attention by his heroes.

I'd first developed an association with the Collingwood Football Club after I gave their staff and players a talk on resilience in 2015. A year later I received a bit of an SOS call from Christian Stagliano, head of player welfare at the club. The Magpies had lost three games in a row, Nathan Buckley's job was on the line and the players were particularly flat.

'We need a half-hour pep talk from you,' Stags said. 'Can you talk about things that will cheer the boys up?'

'What do you mean exactly?' I said.

'Oh, y'know, all that good stuff about how there's more to life than footy. We really need them to understand that at the moment.'

'Ohhh,' I said. 'Gratitude and empathy. I've got just the thing for them.'

A few days later I walked into the Collingwood rooms armed with some footage of Beefy's pep talks from cricket training – the boys were always keen to capture and share footage of this motivational genius at work, such is the nature of social media these days. Each related to Beefy's key areas of motivation:

- 'There's more to life than fucking sport! Do you know how many people can't even play sport?'
- 'I'm telling you now, boys, you may have lost a few games, but that doesn't bother me. What bothers me is your level of effort and your attitude.'
- 'There are people sleeping on the side of the road and you're sooking because you can't win a game? Fuck off!'

The Magpies absolutely loved it. I wasn't watching the videos of Beefy; instead I was watching the Collingwood boys. Beefy's deliveries were so good, so passionate, so funny and so emotional that the players went from rolling on the floor laughing one minute to almost weeping the next. It was clear that the message was hitting home.

Afterwards I addressed the team about the power of empathy and the myriad benefits that flow from being kind and loving towards others. In winding up I said, 'Hey boys, just so you know, that guy Beefy is your number-one sup-porter. Do you know what he does with his money? He saves it up so he can afford a flight and accommodation whenever you guys play in Sydney, Brisbane, Adelaide and Perth. He travels with you every single week. Every home game and every away game, Beefy is there for you.'

As I was packing up to leave, Beefy's idol Nathan Buckley walked over to me and said, 'Mate, I'm in.'

'In for what, Bucks?'

'Your whole talk was about empathy, about doing things for other people, and how when you do things for other people it makes you feel good, right? Well, I want to do something for your mate Beefy. I want to organise a surprise for him – something really special.'

I thought Nathan was going to sign a jumper for him, or maybe get the team to sign a jumper *and* a footy for him. But instead Nathan said, 'Do you reckon Beefy would like to be our water boy for a day?'

'Bucks, I kid you not,' I said, 'that would make his life.'

Nathan pretty much had a plan figured out already. He would send out an urgent call for a Collingwood water boy and have Beefy be at the centre of it.

'One more thing,' Nathan said before I left. 'Would Beefy want to give us one of his motivational speeches?'

'Oh, no-no-no-no! He would shit himself, mate!' I said. I didn't want Beefy to be too overwhelmed. 'Maybe best to just go with water boy for a day.'

Nathan was adamant. 'No, if I think he's up to it, I'm going to get him to do it.'

'Oh, please don't.'

'No, Hugh, we're playing Carlton. They're our biggest rivals. We're doing it.'

As Magpies training kicked off at the Holden Centre the following Wednesday, I picked Beefy up at Richmond Station. I'd told him we were going to take a walk around the Botanical Gardens, which just happened to be nearby. He'd been in the car for a couple of minutes when my phone rang. I put it on speaker.

'Hello, Hugh speaking.'

'G'day Hugh. It's Tarkyn Lockyer, assistant coach at Collingwood Football Club. How are you going?' (Tarkyn was one of Beefy's all-time favourite players.)

'Oh, hey! How are you, Tarkyn? This is a bit of a surprise,' I said, and gave Beefy a 'Can you believe it?' look.

'Well, I'm calling in a favour,' Tarkyn explained. 'I might need your help.'

'Oh yeah, what's happened?'

'We're just about to head out for training and we've

found out we're a couple of water boys short. We actually need some help.'

'You need someone to run water at training? Mate, I'm in the car right now with Beefy. Do you remember how I spoke about Beefy last week? He runs water for our cricket club.'

I turned to Beefy and asked, 'Mate, would you be interested in doing it?' The look on his face was priceless. He was all choked up and shaking his head in disbelief, but still trying to act cool about it.

'Yeah, sure,' Beefy said. He now had a massive grin.

I told Tarkyn, 'Mate, you won't believe this, we're literally driving down Swan Street at the moment. We could be there in two minutes.'

'Oh, mate, that would be amazing,' said Tarkyn, sounding relieved. 'We just need a hand for training. We desperately need someone.'

I turned back to Beefy to make sure he was up for it. 'Are you in?' I said. I thought he was going to cry.

'Yeah! No worries. Yes!'

'Are you sure?'

'Yes!' he barked back impatiently.

I said goodbye to Tarkyn and hung up. A minute or so later we arrived at Magpies HQ. Beefy couldn't get out of the car quick enough, and I have never seen him walk so fast. He zeroed in on Collingwood training as if the scene might disappear in a puff of smoke at any moment. He had an opportunity to run water for his idols and he wasn't going to miss it.

The Magpies were lovely. They kitted Beefy out in an official fluorescent runner's vest and introduced him around. Star ruckman Brodie Grundy walked straight up to him and shook his hand. 'Beefy,' he said, 'it's a pleasure to meet you.'

Next, captain Scott Pendlebury jogged over and introduced himself: 'Beefy, welcome to the club, mate. We're so happy to have you.' Before long, players were running up to him from left, right and centre to put an arm around his shoulder and shake his hand.

Beefy had died and gone to footy heaven, but I could also see he was mystified as to how everybody seemed to know who he was. It didn't matter one bit – if you give Beefy an opportunity in life, he'll grab it with both hands and pull it in close. Pretty soon he'd made himself right at home.

I have to admit that my heart was in my mouth when Nathan Buckley walked over and introduced himself. In Beefy's black-and-white Collingwood-obsessed world, it was akin to having God himself descend from a cloud to personally shake your hand and ask you how your day was going.

Nathan went even further. He gave Beefy a tour of the club and pulled back the curtain on the 'inner sanctum' stuff that Beefy loves and considers to be sacred ground: the change rooms, the gym, the rehab facilities and the team meeting room. Beefy tried to come off like he was on top of it all, that he was cool and fine with everything, but I knew he wasn't. He was blown away.

Back out on the oval, Beefy ran water as the boys went through their paces. Collingwood was due to face old foes Carlton at the MCG in four days' time and – after a rough first half of the season – the stakes were pretty high. All of a sudden Nathan Buckley called the squad into a huddle.

'Gentlemen,' he said, 'we've got Beefy here today. He's a well-known motivational speaker and we're lucky to have him. So, Beefy, have you got any words of motivation for us?'

They say 'Cometh the hour, cometh the man': Beefy stepped into the huddle and delivered one of his finest ever sporting addresses.

'Oh yeah, so you're playing Carlton?' he began. 'Yeah, they've won a few games, they carry on. Who gives a shit? Oh, you've won some games? Well done!'

The team started to lift; they were laughing, but I could see they were also getting the same tingles that our cricket club got every time Beefy gathered us in close.

'So this weekend,' Beefy said as he built to his crescendo, 'you go out there, you hit 'em hard, you bury them and tell them how shit they really are!'

An almighty cheer erupted as the players soared high on the words of Australia's best motivational speaker. They mobbed Beefy, scuffed up his head, hugged him tight and shook him so much that his hat fell off. When they headed for the change rooms Beefy was left standing in the middle of the oval with his hat askew, his hair all messed up and a smile from ear to ear. He turned to Nathan Buckley and said, 'Is that what you wanted?'

Nathan smiled and replied, 'It was perfect, mate. Disrespect the opposition. I love it!'

Four days later, the Magpies beat Carlton by two goals and broke their losing streak. I spoke to Nathan Buckley about the team's turnaround the following week.

'I tell you what,' he said, 'this isn't the reason we won, but when I turned up to the game the players were in a totally different headspace. I was too. I just felt so good about what we'd done as a club, what we were able to provide this young man with, and there's something very powerful in that.'

We chatted for a bit about the importance of having empathy, making strong connections and investing yourself in the wellbeing of others. Then Nathan said, 'What's Beefy doing this weekend? We're playing Greater Western Sydney at home and they're going to be hard to beat.'

I laughed because I thought he was joking.

'I'm serious, Hugh. Do you reckon he'd want to come to Sydney with us for the weekend?'

A few days later Beefy flew to Sydney with the Magpies, where they beat the GWS Giants by 32 points. They even invited him to bring his mum and dad along, and offered to take them into the change rooms after the game.

'We couldn't believe it,' Beefy's mum told me later. 'All the players were going straight up to Nick, cuddling him and high-fiving him. They're his heroes and they were hugging *him* and shouting out *his* name! We can't believe what's happened, Hugh. What have you done?'

'I haven't done anything, Mrs Burke,' I told her. 'Nathan Buckley has done it, and your son has done it.'

Beefy still gets tapped to deliver motivational speeches for the Magpies – particularly when their backs are against the wall. In 2018 they were due to face Richmond in the preliminary final, and no one had given them a chance of winning. On that occasion Beefy opted for his tried-and-tested approach – disrespecting the opposition.

'Oh yeah, fucking Richmond. Oh yeah, they won a flag! Well I'm a bit sick of how smarmy they've become,' Beefy began.

The rest is history. Collingwood beat Richmond by 39 points and advanced to the grand final.

My own journey with Beefy had begun when I was experiencing a personal nadir. I couldn't move on from the death of my granny or my failed relationship with Anjali, but the connection with Beefy gave me something else to think about, not least his pump-ups at training and seeing him at cricket on the weekend.

Pretty soon I went from thinking, 'Oh, poor me and my terrible breakup' to 'How's Beefy's going? Just look at him! He's had an unbelievable time today. He's ten feet tall! He's strutting around and he's happy.'

Our bond may have started out on a teacher/student basis, but we've come a long, long way since. Beefy is one of my closest and dearest friends. We still have a bit of a teacher/student relationship, only now we've swapped roles. Beefy has taught me so much.

It was fitting that Beefy was front and centre when I

promised my undying devotion to the true love of my life, my amazing bride Penny. When we married in early 2019 we asked Beefy to be the co-master of ceremonies and, of course, to say a few motivational words as we embarked on our life together.

'Oh yeah, so you're married now, are ya?' he began. 'Well, just remember this – no complacency. You've just gotta commit!'

CHAPTER 12

GOING PUBLIC

By mid-2019, The Resilience Project had delivered mental wellbeing programs to more than 1400 private, government and independent schools around the country, of which I'd personally worked with more than a thousand. In addition to the NRL and the AFL, we'd worked with the Australian women's netball team, the Diamonds, every A-League soccer club and more than 500 businesses. I was deeply fulfilled by all of this, but I was also totally and utterly exhausted.

Nothing underscored my exhaustion more than when, in 2016, I collapsed mid-talk in front of 250 parents at a primary school. My schedule had been booked out the previous couple of years, and in that year alone I delivered more than 600 talks across the country and abroad. On this occasion, I remember feeling dizzy, but given I was presenting on resilience I told myself to soldier on. Then the scary bit happened: my vision went blurry. I tried to persevere, but before I knew it I had collapsed onto the stage. Now that's an awkward ending for a talk. It was obvious I needed help with the program, though I'd known that deep down for a while.

Every man and his dog was telling me I needed to get another presenter to meet demand. I knew that was easier said than done – we needed someone who connected with the mission of The Resilience Project, and who had charisma and a sense of humour. Someone who could wow six-year-olds, inspire teens and move adults. Oh, and they had to have zero ego. It was a big ask.

To my great surprise, I found someone in the form of Martin Heppell. Martin had also attended Carey Baptist Grammar, six years ahead of me. Although he was gone by the time I arrived, I'd heard stories about this mysterious, legendary character. People spoke about him as if he was a god. Martin's early childhood had been spent living in the jungles of Borneo, where his father, an anthropologist, had relocated the family from Canberra.

When the Heppells returned to Australia, Martin developed into a freakishly talented footballer who was recruited into the AFL straight from high school to play for St Kilda and then Melbourne. His nickname, given to him by the late great St Kilda legend Danny Frawley, was 'Rac' because his hair made him look like a raccoon. Martin only played a couple of seasons at the top level, though; in his words, he was 'an absolute shit kicker'.

Later on Martin became a schoolteacher, and I'd actually bumped into him in the early days of The Resilience Project. He'd been promoted to the role of assistant principal, and in that capacity he introduced me to the students at his school before I went on stage to give a talk.

I was struck by his choice of attire first and foremost: a tweed suit jacket with a shirt and tie, shorts, and a pair of basketball shoes with socks pulled up to his knees. The striking image was accentuated by his shoulder-length hair, which was being temporarily tamed by an upturned terry towelling hat. Without going into specifics, let's just say Martin's way of introducing me was energetic and unique, and well and truly grabbed the attention of the kids.

Martin and I had first crossed paths in 2000, when he came to play with my local amateur football club after his professional career had finished. I had never met a person like him. From the very first game I was in awe of Martin's unstoppable positivity. I'd been dragged from the ground in the first five minutes for screwing up – I can't remember the exact reason, but I would guess it had something to do with my avoiding physical contact. I wasn't the most courageous footballer.

As I was doing the jog of shame off the oval, however, Martin started yelling at my opponent about how fast I was and how, when I came back on, the game was going to change because no one would be able to keep up with me. It was the biggest pump-up I'd ever received in any sporting match, especially considering I'd just been dragged.

I spent the rest of the game watching Martin. As soon as he saw someone looking down or lacking confidence, he was in their face giving them another almighty pump-up about how great they were. I remember admiring him from the bench, thinking, 'Who is this guy?' He was an absolute force of nature.

By 2016, after I'd seen Martin in action at his school, I was in a position where I was able to offer him a job – well, only just. It would have to be half of his current salary for now, I explained, but with a view to growing that down the track. He was still listening, though. I gave him the job out-line: fly around the country, pumping people up and making them feel happier. He was in. And he didn't care about the money.

Despite our expansion into elite sport and the business world, educating schoolchildren remained The Resilience Project's primary focus. For me, schools are the ground zero of the mental health crisis. I was solidly booked a full year in advance for schools alone but I was confident Martin would also be able to reach kids, capture their imagination and equip them with the fundamentals of GEM that are woven into his own amazing life story: learning gratitude from the elders of the tribe he grew up with in Borneo; learning empathy from the kids of the tribe, who took him in and loved him like a brother; learning mindfulness from his formative years spent in the jungle. When you're talking to Martin, he's so present that it's as if you're the only person in the world at that moment.

In his time working as assistant principal, Martin also coached at one of Melbourne's elite football schools, a breeding ground for future AFL stars. One of the first rules he implemented as coach was that the boys' dads weren't allowed in the change rooms after a game unless they hugged their son and told them they loved them. He was worried some of the boys weren't getting enough of that attention and affection at home, so he made sure it happened at footy.

During his first year at The Resilience Project, Martin gave three or four talks a day as he travelled all over the country, often forgoing time with his own two young children because he was so committed to our mission of helping people feel happier. Martin is not your average school wellness program presenter. He's pretty out there; for the first couple of years he was with us he still had long scruffy hair, which is now shaved to a zero. So he looks a bit different, and he has a gravelly voice so he sounds a bit different, too. He can be very, very intense in his presentations, and he's happy to take risks and be candid.

One day Martin phoned me to give a heads-up that I might be about to get some complaints about him. 'I'm really sorry, Hugh,' he said, 'but I've just had an altercation with a teacher.'

'A teacher?' I was surprised, and a bit worried. 'What happened?'

Martin had been conducting a session with a group of teachers at a primary school in Melbourne. One middle-aged male staff member wasn't listening, and was stage-whispering snide comments about Martin to his colleagues.

As part of the session Martin had the teachers write a gratitude letter to someone they really cared about, to thank them for the influence they'd had on their lives. As the 30 or so teachers knuckled down to complete the exercise, the trouble-maker leaned back in his chair against the wall, folded his arms and started laughing and trying to disrupt his colleagues.

'OK,' Martin said. 'Can everybody please put your pens down for a minute?'

When he had their attention, Martin singled out the pest: 'Mate, I don't care if you don't like me. I don't care if you don't respect me, but do not ever show this lack of courtesy to your colleagues ever again.

'Have you noticed that no one is on board with what you're doing? You need to apologise to your colleagues for being so disrespectful to them and what they're trying to achieve today. I reckon now is a good time to do that, but if you're not brave enough to do it right away, just make sure you get it done at some point.'

When he finished telling me the story I imagined the phones back at the office melting under the heat of incoming complaints from angry teachers. I needn't have worried, though, because Martin's judgement of the situation had been spot on. I received just one response, an anonymous email about the incident from a senior teacher:

'I've been at this school for twenty-five years – my entire teaching career,' she wrote. 'The staff member who Martin confronted is terribly arrogant. He's also a lazy teacher, and whenever a guest speaker comes in he makes a point of being rude to them. Please pass on the staff's thanks and appreciation to Martin. It was a wonderful and valuable session, and I have never seen anyone be put in their place so beautifully before. Hopefully it sank in.'

With Martin charging around the country delivering his own special take on GEM, I had a little more time to carry the message of wellbeing further into the community through talks to businesses both big and small.

Over the years I have given presentations for firms ranging from large multinationals – petrochemical giants, mining companies – and big government agencies to a cosmetic company, law firms, retailers and big teams of tradies. I have relished the chance to help make even more people feel happier, and I've felt privileged to meet such a wide cross-section of society and hear the personal stories my fellow Australians might not otherwise share. Based on my observations from very early in the process, it seems that we're all touched in some way by mental illness, if not our own then in someone we love.

People in some industries do it tougher than others. A few years back I delivered a talk to a FIFO mining community in far north Queensland. Men would fly into the remote region to work in the mines for three weeks at a time, then fly back home for nine days to be with their families before heading back to the mines for another three-week stint. The relentless, brutal schedule led to high rates of anxiety and depression.

I told these men my stories about Stanzin and Georgia, and spoke to them about GEM and the benefits of recording three things they were grateful for every day. It was often tough to break through at these talks, where the audience was made up of hard-as-nails, solitary types of men. A year after my first talk, though, I was invited back, since more workers had joined the expanding operation. As I was leaving the second talk, one of the miners followed me outside.

'Sorry, I just want to speak to you before you go if that's OK,' he said.

'Of course, mate,' I said. 'No worries.'

'When I heard a year ago that you were coming to talk to us about mental health, resilience and wellbeing, I couldn't have thought of anything I wanted to sit through less,' he said. 'I was brought in kicking and screaming by my wife. I spent the first forty-five minutes sulking but I actually kind of liked it in the end, and I decided to do that "three things that went well" bit. I have to tell you, it has single-handedly –'

he paused, and looked like he was about to start crying – 'it's single-handedly saved my marriage.'

He said the separation that FIFO enforced on his family had pushed his home life onto a knife's edge: 'Had you asked me back then if my marriage would survive, I'd have said no.'

Every time he sat down to write the three things that went well during the day, however, he realised his wife figured in at least one of them: how hard she worked to look after their children while he was away for three weeks, how she put up with his foul moods during the time he was at home, the sacrifices she'd made to be in his life . . .

'Every night it was something to do with her,' he continued. 'Then I found myself – for the first time in six years – actually missing her when I was down the mines. I can tell you now, our relationship has never been better.'

'Mate, that's the reason I do this,' I told him. 'I'm away from my family right now and standing here with you instead because I know this works! When you practise gratitude every day, you elevate your mood and improve your mental health. Your mental state continues to improve the more you do it. What's happened is you're now scanning the world for positives.'

I didn't start The Resilience Project for accolades, applause or pats on the back – I did it because I believe we can all live happier lives. But I have to admit I love hearing stories from people who have turned their lives around through the application of GEM principles.

Recently I was approached by a young woman after I gave a presentation to a group of real estate agents. 'I saw you speak two years ago,' she said, and began to cry. 'I have a brother with a disability and I've always been a bit angry at him for that. I was just pissed off at how much of an imposition the disability was in our lives, and how hard it was to have a proper relationship with him.'

She described the challenge she faced, being distant from her family because of her attitude, and how no one understood why she was never around. I thought of my early responses to Georgia's battle with anorexia.

'Anyway, I saw your talk,' she said. 'You told us, "Gratitude is when you pay attention to what you've got, not what you don't have." It hit me like a lightning bolt. I realised what I have – I have a brother. I have a *brother*! How lucky am I? I went home that night and I was totally different with him. Now we have an incredible relationship because I have him and he has me – all of me.'

Some crowds, however, can be trickier to engage. Particularly when workers are made to attend a talk their employer thinks is a good idea but they disagree. Some of my more challenging days have involved speaking to groups of tradies employed by a major construction company. I travelled to various depots around Victoria and sometimes had to give an address to a room of blokes at 6.30 am, before they'd even started their work day.

One morning I was about to enter the common room at one such depot when the site manager, my contact for the day, texted to say he couldn't make it. 'Just go ahead and launch into the session as planned,' he wrote. 'The boys will all be there. You'll be fine.'

I walked into the room and said 'G'day boys', only to be met with several dozen men in high-vis keeping their backs turned to me while they tucked into their breakfast of sausage rolls and iced coffees.

'Anyway,' I continued, 'where should I set up?'

'Mate, we don't give a fuck where you set up,' one of the workers drawled, as a few others sniggered.

I was wearing a hoodie with The Resilience Project logo emblazoned across it and as I set up my laptop and a screen to show my slides, one of the boys chimed in with his assessment of the yet-to-be-started session: 'The Gay Project!' he called out.

He got a big laugh for that, which prompted another guy to offer his thoughts: 'Resilience Gay!' That resulted in another burst of throaty laughter. A third fellow thundered: 'Gay Resilience Project!' It brought the house down.

I was torn between my initial thought – to lecture these men on how inappropriate and offensive their language was – and my desire to connect with them in order to get my message across. I decided to kill two birds with one stone: 'Righto – pipe down, ya homophobic motherfuckers!'

There was a three-second silence and a collective look of shock, then the room erupted with laughter. We were up and away.

That session is still one of the most powerful I've ever conducted. At one point, when a couple of the men were opening up about their personal struggles, half the room were in tears. While it's always a pleasure to work with sports stars, there is no greater sense of accomplishment than reaching a group of people who initially don't want to be reached.

We were being inundated with emails from people wanting to know how they could hear from us if their workplace or school weren't hosting one of my talks, so I began to develop the idea of speaking to the general public about happiness. In 2015, I booked the 800-seat ACMI theatre in Federation Square and was blown away when we sold out two nights.

The first night was shaky and my presentation full of stutters, as I struggled with nerves and impostor syndrome. On the second night I loosened up as I realised I could be more myself at public events. I wasn't representing a school or speaking to a business, so I didn't have to be as conservative with what I said.

Given the number of people who were clearly motivated to do something about improving their mental health and wellbeing, we took the plunge and booked the Melbourne Convention Centre in 2017. I was nervous; surely we weren't going to sell out a 2500-seat venue. Much to my astonishment, we sold it out three times over. Off the back of that, we booked a national tour and presented the talk in sold-out major venues around Australia, reaching tens of thousands of people in a matter of a few months. And, in 2019, we sold out every gig on my national tour.

My idols growing up were mostly sports stars: Michael Jordan, Steve Waugh, Andrew Gaze. But another hero of mine, someone my whole family worshipped, was the comedian Billy Connolly. This was a man who stood on stage and told stories that made people happy. Over the years I studied his every move and every word. I loved how vulnerable and imperfect he allowed himself to be. The more experience I've had with big crowds and sold-out venues, the more I've felt the kind of out-of-body experience you hear people describe of their experiences on stage. I think they call it flow: in my case, I find myself sitting back and watching the performance, like anyone else in the audience. I think to myself, 'I'm telling stories to make people feel happier. This is a pretty cool job.'

The public talks always end up being fairly late nights; as in the mining fields of Queensland, the locker rooms of AFL clubs and the staffrooms of schools around the country, people like to tell me their personal stories after I finish. It's a part of the night I love, and sometimes I even get a special surprise.

After a talk at the Melbourne Convention Centre in early 2019, a queue formed of people wishing to have a chat with me or give me a hug. Finally, as I worked my way to the end of the queue, I found myself standing face to face with three young women. I thought I recognised them . . . sort of. It wasn't until they started talking that the penny dropped. They were my Year 5 students from Fintona Girls School, all grown up.

'Hi sir! How are you?' one of them said, beaming.

'Oh my God, Lippy!' I exclaimed. 'What are you guys doing here?'

'We heard about the stuff you were doing and we weren't

going to miss it,' Lippy said. 'I don't know what all the fuss is about,' she said with a massive smile. 'I was going to yell out, "Hey, what's symmetry?"'

'Well, this is weird!' I said. 'Look at you guys all grown up. Do you remember the Little Lad Dance?'

'What do you think?' Lippy said, before performing the entire rendition.

CHAPTER 13
A QUICK WORD ON BUSINESS

The Resilience Project has grown rapidly. Nowadays we have a staff of 11 working on helping people find happiness through GEM principles. When you consider the World Health Organization has predicted that by 2030 depression will be the number-one health concern in both developed and developing nations, you realise the task ahead is enormous.[1]

Over recent years, we've met this challenge head-on by becoming a bona fide professional outfit rather than a one-man show run on pure belief and the funds of 'minus one coffee'. But our status as a business is something I struggle with every day. I look at The Resilience Project as more of a service or a movement than a business or commercial enterprise, and I have to remind myself when I make tough decisions in the organisation's financial best interests that it's to enable us to keep fulfilling our purpose.

Years ago the 'staff' was just me, and the 'office' was a desk in my bedroom in a share house. I was hopeless at sending invoices and just as hopeless at chasing up outstanding bills. I recall sitting in my room one night with a spreadsheet listing all the schools I'd visited and one of my friends remarking, 'You know you can get a program that helps you manage your clients.'

I know he was just trying to give me a little business advice, but the words he used were jarring. I could no sooner stand in rooms full of children, teenagers, parents, teachers or professionals and think of them as clients than I could fly to the moon. I decided I would never have 'clients': I would have friends instead. And I certainly wouldn't 'manage' them; I would have relationships with them.

This was not just an exercise in semantics; I believe I owe it to all the people I work with to treat them as I treat my friends. I listen to them, help them out when I can, am honest with them and never ignore them. When things do go wrong on the job, I've found the best thing is to pick up the phone and call the person straight away and absolutely own every second of what has happened.

I have developed some great relationships with at least one staff member from many of the schools I've worked in. One of the first primary schools I visited, for example, had us implement a comprehensive resilience training program, and over time I became good mates with the principal, a lovely man named Eric. Rather than pack up and leave straight after a presentation I would always go and hang out in Eric's office. He loved to chat about what was going on in the school and the sorts of issues he was dealing with as a principal.

The head of wellbeing at the same school also became a good friend. We stayed in touch and still message each other from time to time. That school has done so much to support The Resilience Project; they believed in us from the start and even let us film promotional material on the grounds.

One day, the head of wellbeing and I were chatting on the phone when she mentioned a speaker they'd organised to present to their staff had cancelled. 'Can you recommend anyone?'

'Yeah, I can do it.'

She baulked a little. 'We don't have a huge amount left in our budget.'

'No, I meant I'll do it for free,' I said. If a friend is in need of a helping hand, you just give it to them. I lost count of the number of talks I did for free in the early years. In my experience with the business, I've found that if you use as the primary measure of success how much you're improving people's lives, as opposed to how much money you're making, the former will take care of the latter in the long term.

As we've grown over the past few years, a lot of people have wanted to give me business advice and some have even offered to be my 'business coach'. Almost without fail the first thing they ask me is, 'What's your five-year plan? Where do you want to be in five years' time? Where do you see yourself in ten years?'

I don't have a five-year plan; I have a moment-by-moment plan. My plan is to give every moment I am in my full and undivided attention, whether it's with my family or friends, at schools or with sports teams or businesses. I don't sit around planning out the future; we spend so much time worrying about what might happen, but when you think about it, the future never really 'arrives', because by the time it does it's already become the present. My advice is: wherever you are, be there. It's my belief that if you can invest all your effort in the present moment, then the longer term will take care of itself.

I take the same attitude with people. When you have the privilege of spending time with another person, be totally in that moment. So many people these days are looking for someone better to talk to; they're looking at their phone, or their minds are wandering. I don't want to be like that. When I'm with someone I want them to feel like it's just me and them: that there's no one else there, and there's nothing I'd rather be doing than engaging with them.

As a consequence, I have to admit I have a real problem with time. I'm constantly late, mainly because I don't want to shorten any moment I'm experiencing. If something is going well, I don't like wrapping it up. Besides, I'd rather be late and available than punctual and anxious to get away from people as soon as possible.

Another thing that I hope sets me apart from the average business owner is the fact I don't care how much money we make. You could argue that someone would only have that attitude if money wasn't a problem, but beyond knowing that we make enough to keep pushing the principles of GEM to as many people as we can, I couldn't care less what the balance sheet shows. What matters to me far more is whether or not I'm fulfilling my purpose.

Purpose is not always what you think it is. When I started working with Port Adelaide Football Club I asked the players, 'What's your purpose?' They'd tell me things like, 'Get picked in the team. Win a grand final. Win a Brownlow Medal.'

'That's not your purpose,' I'd point out, 'that's a goal. Yes, we need to have goals, but our purpose sits outside of those specific aims and outcomes. What if you get injured the next day? You can't play finals, you can't win a Brownlow, so what's your purpose? What are you getting out of bed for each day?' Sometimes it takes us a while to discover what that is.

My purpose is simply to help people be happier. When The Resilience Project wasn't doing well financially early on I didn't get down about it, because I knew that making money wasn't my purpose. So long as I was still able to get up the next morning and help people improve their well-being, then I was perfectly happy. I should have been more responsible about the money side of things, but I believe the organisation's clear sense of motivation has helped us from a business point of view, in tangible and intangible ways.

Without a five-year plan to follow, our expansion has happened organically and largely through word of mouth. Recently, that word has been heard overseas. In 2020, The Resilience Project is going into schools in New Zealand and we now have a partnership with some schools in the UK.

It's daunting, and I'm not sure how we're going to manage. If it works, though, I'll be over the moon, because the GEM method will be spreading far and wide.

CHAPTER 14

ON FACING CRITICS

'The Resilience Project is a cult!'

These six words were the last I'd been expecting to hear – in a school hall, no less! I had arrived early one evening for a presentation to parents at a school in Melbourne. As the parents were starting to arrive, I got chatting with the student wellbeing officer.

'We're expecting a pretty big turnout tonight,' she told me. 'About four hundred people are coming, but I can tell you there's one parent who won't be here.'

'Oh yeah?' I said. 'Why so?'

She explained how the irate mother of a student had come to the school earlier in the week to lodge a complaint about The Resilience Project. This mum was totally opposed to our curriculum, which runs throughout the year, and having to pay for the books so her child could take part. 'Just to let you know, I will not be buying The Resilience Project curriculum,' she told the teacher. 'And I want my child to be out of the class whenever the program is being taught.'

The teacher had asked for her reasons.

'Because The Resilience Project is a cult,' the mum said.

'Well, it's not *really* a cult,' the teacher replied. 'But if that's how you feel, you should come along to the parents' night.'

'I don't need to listen to a cult leader speak!' the mother had apparently snapped back.

Just as the teacher was relaying this story to me, the lady in question turned up, and the teacher pointed her out. She sat in the front row, folded her arms and stared daggers at me.

I always spend the first five minutes of any talk trying to do two things: connect with the audience and make people laugh. I noticed that within two minutes, the concerned mother was laughing along with the rest of the audience. When she heard the story of Georgia's battles with mental illness, and the way that GEM practice had made an impact on her life, I could tell from the way she was looking at me that she understood I wasn't a cult leader with sinister intentions. For the rest of the night, she had her pen and paper out and was taking notes.

The thing is, I expect to be judged. I'm not infallible: I don't have all the answers, I don't pretend to be a psychologist, and I'm not trying to brainwash anyone. When it boils down to it, The Resilience Project is simply presenting, in an entertaining way, evidence-based ways to feel happier.

Strip away the emotional talks, the slideshows and the background research, and we are simply educating people in how to be kind to others, be mindful of the world around them and be grateful for the things that go well for them. Nor is The Resilience Project by any means the only organisation out there trying to help people improve their wellbeing. We're simply having discussions with people around the country about mental health, and advocating for what the research shows: if you practise GEM, you should feel happier.

We have come in for criticism from time to time, mostly from people who haven't been to a presentation of ours and who happen to work in the field with their own well-established programs. My view is that the mental health and wellbeing space should be collaborative rather than competitive. The rates of mental illness in this country right now are devastating; the more we work together, the more we can achieve.

Andrew Wallis, a physiotherapist at St Kilda Football Club, explained to me the need for collaboration in tackling mental health really well: 'When I'm presented with a player who has an injury, I go and speak to the sports doctor. I work with the strength and conditioning specialists at the club, the nutritionist, the masseur – you name it,' he said. 'There are four or five of us working on this injury together. We all come from very different areas – prevention, rehab, surgery, physiotherapy – but we work together. The same collaborative approach should apply with mental health.'

In fact, it was after our work with the nations' top football clubs attracted publicity that I encountered some of this exact kind of reflexive pushback from a couple of sports psychologists. The thing is, though, I'm not diagnosing anyone, nor am I trying to treat anyone's mental illness. I'm just telling a few stories and encouraging people to be kind to each other, to be grateful for the things they have and to practise meditation. I've never had sports players, schoolkids, professionals or anyone else 'on the couch', so to speak, and I've been very careful not to stray outside of my lane or pretend I know more than I do. I've been employing this approach since my days teaching primary school, when students would seek me out as a sounding board. I never gave them advice, I never probed, but I always listened to them.

I found myself doing the same thing at sporting clubs. I've lost count of how many times players have sought me out to unburden themselves of sometimes deep, serious mental issues. I will always listen to them but, without fail, I tell them, 'Mate, I'm not a psychologist. You need to speak to a qualified psychologist, because they are the people who are best equipped to help you.'

Although some sports psychologists have had their reservations about me at first, I've had great support from the vast majority of them – especially once they've met me and listened to my presentation.

As much as I tried to shrug the criticism off, it would still get me down at times. Finally I found comfort in an excerpt from a speech that former US President Theodore Roosevelt gave in 1910, the speech made famous by Brené Brown, a research professor at the University of Houston. The passage, which deals with how one faces criticism, is widely known as 'The Man in the Arena':

> It is not the critic who counts; not the man who points out how the strong man stumbles, or where the doer of deeds could have done them better. The credit belongs to the man who is actually in the arena, whose face is marred by dust and sweat and blood; who strives valiantly; who errs, who comes short again and again, because there is no effort without error and shortcoming; but who does actually strive to do the deeds; who knows great enthusiasms, the great devotions; who spends himself in a worthy cause; who at the best knows in the end the triumph of high achievement, and who at the worst, if he fails, at least fails while daring greatly, so that his place shall never be with those cold and timid souls who neither know victory nor defeat.

In other words: 'If you're going to have the courage to create something and put yourself out there, there will be people who want to have a crack at you. It's inevitable. But if you're not in the arena with me, fighting alongside me,

I don't care what you think. Your "feedback" is of no interest to me.' I found the quote very empowering.

I got chatting about it to Travis Boak, the former captain of the Port Adelaide Football Club. As an elite sportsperson, he's on centre stage in front of hundreds and thousands of people; he puts himself out there every single day. He is a phenomenal footballer and, without fail, he comes in for an avalanche of criticism. In the past he would get down about it, but now he writes 'Man in the Arena' on his boots.

When I give a presentation, I'm always holding a remote control that allows me to click through the slides I'm referencing. I took a leaf out of Travis's book and wrote 'MITA' (for Man in the Arena) on the back of my clicker. I'm not usually one for inspirational quotes, but this one has helped to make me feel bulletproof. The best approach to dealing with critics, as they say, is to 'kill them with success and bury them with a smile'. That saying has inspired me on so many occasions to move beyond petty complaints and insecure 'feedback', and to work even harder to succeed.

None of this is to say I am above criticism, or that I'm not willing to broaden my knowledge and improve what we do at The Resilience Project. We are always keen to improve our work, and feedback is key to that of course. For that reason, we have agreed to a comprehensive three-year evaluation with Melbourne University. My hope is that they can provide evidence that what we're doing in communities around the country is having a positive impact on people's mental health. At the very least, the evaluation will provide us with exceptional feedback on how we can get better in order to help more people.

Over the years, word of mouth about The Resilience Project has given me some amazing opportunities I never dreamed were possible. In September 2016 I received a phone call from Cricket Australia. Management had got wind of our work with the NRL and AFL, and they wanted me to give an address to the Australian players.

'This,' I told myself as I put down the phone, 'is going to be the greatest honour of my life.'

My talk was scheduled for two months later in Brisbane, where the team would be preparing for their upcoming Test series. For the best part of eight weeks, the prospect of working with the Australian cricket team was almost all I could think about.

As a bonus, one of my closest mates, Grant Baldwin, happened to be the team masseur, so I was excited about catching up with 'Baldy', too. In all, it promised to be a great trip personally and professionally. I know what a gruelling mental game cricket can be, so I was eager to offer the team some tools that would help them be happier not only in their sport but also in their personal lives.

The address was locked in for nine o'clock on a Sunday morning. As I boarded the plane for Brisbane on the Saturday afternoon I realised I wasn't the slightest bit nervous. All I felt was excitement for what I was planning to be the best talk I'd ever given.

Baldy had told me to come and see him as soon as I landed, so on Saturday evening I made my way over to his hotel in the Brisbane CBD. I'd barely walked through the door before he asked if I wanted to get a beer.

'Baldy, I actually can't drink the night before a talk,' I demurred. 'It sounds silly, but it's a rule I stick to.'

As a public speaker I know alcohol leaves me with a reduced capacity for fluency the following day – even if I have just one drink the night before. That's the reason for my golden rule: 'Never drink a drop the night before a talk.' It has served me well.

'Just one beer!' Baldy said, palms upturned pleadingly.

'Even if it's just one or two beers, I wouldn't be at my best tomorrow,' I dug in.

'I'm only saying one beer though!'

Geez, Baldy was awfully thirsty. Still, I kept pushing back: 'I'd rather not, mate.'

That's when he pulled out his trump card. Baldy adopted a serious tone and said, 'Listen, mate, my ex-girlfriend moved in with her new boyfriend today and I just want to go and have a beer with you.'

I love Baldy, and I've always felt it's a privilege to be mates with him. And anyway, he had me at 'ex-girlfriend'.

'OK,' I said. 'One beer. Just one!'

Fifteen minutes later, Baldy and me and my rubber arm were nursing a pint in a noisy, crowded pub just down the road from his hotel. 'Geez, there's plenty happening here,' Baldy said after a few sips on his beer. 'I'd prefer a quiet drink somewhere else.'

'Well, you'll be doing it on your own,' I thought, 'because I'm out of here in a minute.'

We were halfway through our beers when Steve Smith, the then Australian cricket captain, suddenly appeared with a couple of other players. I tried to play it cool, but that was proving difficult – I hadn't loved a cricketer this much since Ricky Ponting, and before him Steve Waugh. I was in the presence of greatness, and was almost speechless as Baldy introduced me to one of my personal heroes.

Steve Smith was as genuine and humble as they come. I was blown away by how interested he was in *my* cricket at the Melbourne University Cricket Club. Here I was, talking with one of the game's great players of our time, and he wanted to know where my team was on the ladder, what our home wicket was like, which young players we had coming through the ranks. The guy's love of cricket was clear as day.

'I can't wait for tomorrow,' Steve told me. 'So many of my mates have seen you in action, and every one of them says I have to hear your talk. So I really can't wait, Hugh. Anyway . . . what are you drinking, mate? Can I get you one?'

'Ohh,' I said as Baldy flashed me a mocking grin. 'I was just going to have the one, Steve, but . . . OK, a pot – no a pint – wait, yes, a pint please.' I kicked myself at the awkward explosion of yes and no and pots and pints.

Steve disappeared and returned with the promised pint for me and Baldy.

Suddenly I was two beers deep.

Steve and Baldy were excellent company. I've always loved the flow and rhythm of a pub, when you have a pint in your hand and find yourself in the presence of great storytellers. As I finished my second pint the Australian captain was momentarily distracted by someone else in the pub so I leaned over and told Baldy, 'Mate, I might duck off now. It's already ten o'clock and I need to be fresh for tomorrow.'

'It's important for you to get to know Steve,' Baldy retorted. 'I don't think you should walk away. The Australian cricket captain just bought you a drink! Are you not going to buy him one back?'

And with that challenge I arrived at the dreaded cross-roads. Looking back I should have taken the route that led straight to the bar, bought Steve his drink, given it to him and said, 'There you go, mate. Great to meet you. I'll see you again in the morning.' But I didn't. I came back from the bar with a drink for Steve and another pint each for me and Baldy.

Three beers deep.

Twenty minutes later, Steve left but a few members of the Australian top order came and joined us. They were such a lovely group of young men. Many laughs and many great stories later, I sank onto the bed in my hotel room, completely off my chops. I lowered my head into my hands. 'What the fuck have you done?' I mumbled to myself.

Desperately hoping to somehow pull myself together, I set my alarm for seven o'clock and promised myself I'd go for a five-kilometre run along the Brisbane River before proceedings began. 'It'll be hot,' I told myself. 'You'll sweat it all out.'

The next morning, I was still under the influence. So much so that, instead of stopping at the two-and-a-half-kilometre mark and doubling back to the hotel, I continued for five straight kilometres. I stood there proudly for a second, hand on hips, until I realised what I'd done.

'Right, looks like this is going to be a ten-kilometre run in nearly one hundred per cent humidity. This is going to feel like a marathon. Great,' I scolded myself again. Even though I ran the ten kilometres and sweated like a pig, the exercise did nothing to rewire the sluggish circuitry that connected my brain to my mouth.

I had never before put myself in that position. In six years of public speaking – whether addressing a classroom full of students or a group of CEOs – I had *never* had a drink the night beforehand. I thought it was disrespectful to the people who came to hear me speak. If people took time out of their day to listen to what I had to say, they deserved to have me at my very best.

Try telling that to wide-eyed, starstruck cricket tragic Hugh, who couldn't help himself when the captain of the national team said, 'Are you having another one, mate?'

I arrived at the team's hotel conference room with plenty

of time to spare, and who should already be there but Steven Smith, sitting in the front row. He had a pen and a notebook on his lap and he looked as fresh as a daisy. 'G'day, Hugh! Wasn't last night good?' he said, smiling broadly.

'It was good,' was all I could manage.

The other players trickled in. At the stroke of 9 am they closed the doors – and my worst nightmare began. There was no fresh air in the room, and within minutes I started to sweat profusely. I'd worn a grey T-shirt, and I could only cringe as dark, beery wet patches appeared all over my torso.

As my head began to spin, my inner voice warned me, 'Oooh, I'm not too good here. I'm feeling pretty hungover.' When I went to use my outer voice, I almost wished I hadn't. My opening joke, which is usually a well-crafted story, fell flat in front of the Aussies. I completely butchered the timing and clarity. No one laughed. I'll never forget the looks on some of their faces: a look of utter confusion.

If these things could be measured, I was registering near-zero in verbal fluency. I couldn't get into my normal flow and, despite willing myself to get back on track, I messed up story after story. Throughout the talk I kept glancing at my mate Baldy. Long gone was the cheeky grin from the night before. He looked stressed. I think he'd pumped my talk up a lot, and instead of focusing on bringing the talk back to life, I was distracted by my belief that Baldy was now regretting advocating for me.

When it was finally over I received an awkward smattering of semi-applause. I was crushed and all I could think was, 'This was supposed to be my dream come true, and I have completely blown it because I couldn't say no to a drink. Well done.'

I went back to my hotel room and sat slumped against the wall, the way footballers do on the field after losing a big game. And on my way home, I tried to put the whole trip behind me as quickly as possible. I've always said to my own cricket teams, 'A loss isn't a loss. We either have a win or we have a lesson.' On the lonely flight back to Melbourne, I meditated hard on the lesson this time: 'This whole experience is only a disaster if I fail to learn from it.'

When I next met Steve Smith, I was surprised to learn he'd thoroughly enjoyed the presentation. That's when I realised that we are so often our own worst critics. We spend so much time thinking about how others see us, and forget we're not the focus of other people's lives. Particularly a cricket captain's! Regardless, I look forward to one day telling my son that I got to work with one of cricket's all-time greats. It was one of the greatest privileges of my life.

CHAPTER 15

THE FINISH LINE

One thing nagged at me for years. I never knew what happened to Stanzin, the Indian boy whose sense of kindness, happiness and gratitude is at the heart of The Resilience Project. People ask me after every talk, 'What became of Stanzin? What is he up to now?' But I had never been back to the village and so I had no idea what became of him.

In early 2017 I started putting my feelers out. Communication proved difficult. I often thought about jumping on a plane and heading to India, but there was no guarantee I would find him.

In early 2019, however, I managed to make contact with a local teacher who had once worked at the same school. He promised me he would make an effort to find Stanzin for me. Weeks dragged by with no word. Then months.

In June 2019 I was in Darwin to give talks at a series of schools in the Top End. One day I found myself with an hour and a half to kill – the perfect amount of time to do a bit of running. I drove to an athletics centre, changed into my training gear and hit the track. I was halfway through my session when a text message came through on my Apple Watch.

Normally I ignore texts while training, but the number was unfamiliar. The message itself was odd; all it said was 'Hi. Is it.'

I kept running, and a few minutes later another text came through. This time it was one word. 'Hugh.'

As I stood there and puzzled over it, a third message appeared: 'I am Stanzin.'

I was almost in a state of shock. I ran over to where I'd left my bag on the finish line, pulled my phone out and sat straight down on the track. At first I worried it might be a stitch-up from one of my mates, but the messages had clearly come from an overseas number. Then another message came through: 'You gave me a camera when you lived in India. Do you remember? I still have it. Very special.'

I was so excited that my fingers could barely keep up with my racing mind as I typed out a reply. 'Oh Stanzin,' I wrote. 'I'm so excited to hear from you. You're my favourite student I've ever taught in my life. You've inspired me, you've inspired so many people. You're such a special person. Wow! I can't believe I'm speaking to you.'

I sat there nervously awaiting a reply. Would he be happy? Would he understand how much he'd influenced me?

When the reply came through eventually, it was simply stated: 'OK.' I had clearly come in way too hot.

Stanzin told me he'd joined the army and was training in China. He promised me that when he returned home, in December 2019, we'd be able to speak. I told him I looked forward to being in regular contact with him, and that I couldn't wait to hear what had happened over the past eleven years of his life. I'm anxious to tell him what's been going on with me, too, given my experience with him formed such a huge part of my life's purpose.

To be honest, I was always worried that I was a no one in Stanzin's life; that I'd been in it briefly and then he'd forgotten about me. It made me very emotional to think he remembered me.

I couldn't stop smiling as I sat there in the hot Darwin sunshine, exchanging messages with the kindest person I had ever met – the boy who had turned my life around. I chuckled when I noticed I was literally sitting on the finish line, even though I knew it was the start of a whole new chapter for us both.

The other question I am often asked is, 'How is your sister doing these days?' It gives me great joy to be able to answer that question, for my sister is an inspiring story of hope and resilience. When you actually stop and consider what my sister has been through – horrific sexual abuse as a three-year-old, feeling like that sexual abuse was her fault, being told that if anyone knew about the abuse her family would disown her, her subsequent life-threatening mental illness and the devastating impact that illness had on her relationship with her own family – it's almost too heartbreaking to think about. But to see her flourishing now, as a woman in her mid-30s, is an example of hope for anyone who has experienced trauma.

If you ask my sister about the abuse she suffered, her answer truly paints the picture of someone who has not just survived but who has thrived.

'I don't hate the man who did this to me, Hugh,' Georgia has told me. 'I feel sad for him, and I feel great pity for what his life must have been like, in order for him to do that to a child.'

I recall when my sister first said this. 'Are you serious?' I said. My shocked response moved Georgia to go one step further: 'Hugh, I forgive him. Yes, he caused me unspeakable emotional pain, but I'm now at peace with it, and I'm happy about what I'm doing in the world.'

It's hard to keep up with all the incredible stuff my sister is now doing. One thing is for sure: she is the living embodiment of gratitude, empathy and mindfulness. Not because of me or my teachings, though; she has discovered GEM on her own journey. Every night, Georgia writes in her journal the three things that have gone well for her each day, and every morning, she completes a ten-minute meditation.

Georgia's practice of gratitude is deeply rooted in her psyche, and her daily practice of mindfulness enables her to stay calm. As for empathy, I don't know a more empathetic person. It has been the driving force throughout Georgia's adult life. Her every waking second is dedicated to making someone else's life better.

It has actually taken the process of writing this book for me to understand the full power of my sister's recovery. Before I commenced this writing journey, I never quite gave Georgia the credit she deserved for her inspirational resilience. Nor did I understand the full extent to which GEM was at the heart of her recovery.

It wasn't until I sent Georgia the first chapter of this book to read my rendering of her experiences that we were able to talk openly about our relationship. For someone who travels the country presenting about the importance of connection, it was extremely sad and humbling to realise how disconnected I had become from my own sister.

Georgia told me that, ever since that morning in Sydney when we were kids, she had been desperate for connection with me. 'I have always been so jealous of your audience. They get this vulnerable, open and honest connection with you, but I never once got that, despite how desperately I was crying out for it. You chose to be courageous in front of complete strangers, but never once me.'

I thought back over our relationship. It was true that I'd found my sister's attention-seeking embarrassing when we were kids. As a teenager, I'd found her mental illness infuriating. I'd interpreted her move to LA as coming from a need to put distance between her and us, because she didn't care enough.

What I was realising was how uncharitable my response to Georgia's every move had been. All I needed was an honest conversation to understand her actions from her point of view. Georgia wasn't desperate for attention, she was trying to protect us. Her mental illness wasn't her fault, and she'd needed a fresh start in LA.

If it hadn't been for this book, I fear we would still be disconnected. It has taken the writing process for Georgia and me to finally have a conversation that was decades overdue. One thing we've both found, in our own ways, is how important GEM has been in our lives.

I'm not saying that GEM practice is a silver bullet. But just ask little Stanzin: my gosh it makes you feel happier.

ACKNOWLEDGEMENTS

First and foremost, I wish to thank my sister, Georgia, for having the courage and the faith to let me tell her story. While this book has been challenging for both of us, I will always look back on it as the thing that brought us closer together. I am excited about the relationship that we will now have.

Mum, you are the most fiercely loyal and loving person I know. You invested your every waking moment in ensuring Georgia, Josh and I had the best possible childhood. There is no one's approval and affection I seek more. I truly hope this book makes you proud.

Dad, I hope more than anything that I can be half the father you are. I'm yet to meet a nicer person; you're the sweetest and most compassionate man, a wonderful listener and a true joy to be around. You have always been my idol. I know how much you love reading, so I hope you enjoy this.

A huge thank you to my best mate, my little brother Josh. You have been a great sounding board for me throughout this process, the first person I called when I had questions. You've always been that person for me; you have helped me through so many challenges in life with your wisdom and insight. I was only six at the time, but I remember the day you came home from the hospital like it was yesterday. I fell in love instantly.

To my own beautiful family, Penny and Benji, I apologise for the times that the writing process has taken me away from the present moment. Please know that, wherever I am in the world, you are front and centre in my heart and in my mind. Benji, you are the most incredible thing that has ever happened to me. I have never known a love like this before, and you're the inspiration for all that I do. Penny, no one else has had to put up with more throughout the writing process than you have. Thank you for your extraordinary levels of empathy and support. You are the most beautiful person I know.

At The Resilience Project, we are blessed to have the most incredibly hardworking General Manager, Ben Waterman. There is no chance this book would have happened without you, Ben. I was on my last legs when you started with us, and when we agreed to write the book, you moved heaven and earth to allow me the time and space to write. Ben, as much as I love what you've done to The Resilience Project, it's ultimately your friendship I am most grateful for. Your hard work is a constant source of inspiration for me.

A big thank you to all the elite sportspeople who feature throughout the book. It is a hugely courageous decision you have made to have your stories told by someone else. My hope is that your respective journeys will inspire others to feel happy. I feel so honoured to have worked with you all, and I hope you know you have had a significant impact on my life. A special thank you to Marty Kennedy: your story is as raw as it gets. I was exhausted and at the end of my tether when you came and told me what you'd been through. I want you to know that I am still doing my talks because of what you said to me that day.

To Sophie and Tom from Penguin Random House, your patience and guidance has been much appreciated. Thank you for your tireless work. And, of course, thank you for introducing me to Craig.

I was sceptical about the idea of writing this book with someone else – that is, until I met Craig Henderson. Hendo, this book would not have happened without you. For me it was love at first sight in that crowded cafe in Sydney's CBD. I knew instantly that we could work together on this project.

It has been a pleasure to get to know you and your family, and your understanding of emotion and vulnerability has made this process an absolute joy. You are an incredible talent, and I feel privileged to have worked alongside you on this. When I was staying at your house on the NSW South Coast, I asked if you had a favourite surfing memory. Just so you know, my favourite surf is the one we had together, that very afternoon. Thanks, Hendo; this book is as much yours as it is mine.

Finally, to Stanzin. Thank you for everything you've taught me.

NOTES

CHAPTER 3: FINDING PURPOSE

1 See, for example: Szabo, Attila et al., 'Experimental comparison of the psychological benefits of aerobic exercise, humor, and music', *Humor: International Journal of Humor Research*, vol. 18, no. 3, pp. 235–46; Schneider, Martha et al., '"A joke a day keeps the doctor away?" Meta-analytical evidence of differential associations of habitual humor styles with mental health', *Scandinavian Journal of Psychology*, vol. 69, no. 3, pp. 289–300; Panteleeva, Yulia et al., 'Music for anxiety? Meta-analysis of anxiety reduction in non-clinical samples', *Psychology of Music*, vol. 46, no. 4, pp. 473–87; Szabo, Attila et al., 'Effect of spinning workouts on affect', *Journal of Mental Health*, vol. 24, no. 3, pp. 145–9; Barnes, Robert T. et al., 'Evaluating attentional and affective changes following an acute exercise bout using a modified dot-probe protocol', *Journal of Sports Sciences*, vol. 28, no. 10, pp. 1065–76.

CHAPTER 4: THE HAPPIEST BOY ON EARTH

1 For some introductory reading on brain chemistry, social psychology and kindness, see, for example: Pfaff, Donald W., *The Altruistic Brain: How We Are Naturally Good*, Oxford University Press, Oxford, 2015; 'Why kindness heals', James R. Doty, *Huffington Post*, 26 January 2017; 'Hardwired for giving', Elizabeth Svoboda, *Wall Street Journal*, 31 August 2013; 'Acts of kindness: Key to happiness for children and teens', Marilyn Price-Mitchell, *Psychology Today*, 2 January 2013.

CHAPTER 7: MINUS ONE COFFEE

1 'National Health Survey: First results, 2017–18 – mental and behavioural conditions', Australian Bureau of Statistics, 28 May 2019.

2 'National Health Survey: First results, 2017–18 – psychological distress', Australian Bureau of Statistics, 28 May 2019.

3 Seligman, Martin et al., 'Positive psychology progress: Empirical validation of interventions', *American Psychologist*, vol. 60, no. 5, pp. 410–21.

4 See, for example: Emmons, R. A., *Thanks!: How the New Science of Gratitude Can Make You Happier*, Houghton Mifflin Harcourt, Boston, 2007; Emmons, R. A. and McCullough, M. E., 'Counting blessings versus burdens: An experimental investigation of gratitude and subjective well-being in daily life', *Journal of Personality and Social Psychology*, vol. 84, no. 2, pp. 377–89.

5 See, for example: Lanham, Michelle et al., 'How gratitude relates to burnout and job satisfaction in mental health professionals', *Journal of Mental Health Counseling*, vol. 34, no. 4, pp. 341–54; Waters, Lea and Stokes, Helen, 'Positive education for school leaders: Exploring the effects of emotion-gratitude and action-gratitude', *Australian Educational and Developmental Psychologist*, vol. 32, no. 1, pp. 1–22; Chan, David W., 'Burnout and life satisfaction: Does gratitude intervention make a difference among Chinese school teachers in Hong Kong?', *Educational Psychology*, vol. 31, no. 7, pp. 809–23.

6 Toepfer, Steven M. et al., 'Letters of gratitude: Further evidence for author benefits', *Journal of Happiness Studies*, vol. 13, no. 1, pp. 187–201.

7 Jackowska, Marta et al., 'The impact of a brief gratitude intervention on subjective well-being, biology and sleep', *Journal of Health Psychology*, vol. 21, no. 10, pp. 2207–17.

8 Baston, C. Daniel et al., 'Empathy and attitudes: Can feeling for a member of a stigmatized group improve feelings toward the group?', *Journal of Personality and Social Psychology*, vol. 72, no. 1, pp. 105–18.

9 Condon, Paul et al., 'Meditation increases compassionate response to suffering', *Psychological Science*, vol. 24, no. 10, pp. 2125–7. Note: the researchers were careful to make a distinction between compassion and empathy, but because there is a component of empathy (empathetic concern) that is closely related, they cited the study as an example of an empathy intervention.

10 Kerr, Shelly et al., 'Can gratitude and kindness interventions enhance well-being in a clinical sample?', *Journal of Happiness Studies*, vol. 16, no. 1, pp. 17–36.

11 See: Pressman, Sarah et al., 'It's good to do good and receive good: The impact of a "pay it forward" style kindness intervention on giver and receiver well-being', *Journal of Positive Psychology*, vol. 10, no. 4, pp. 293–302; Layous, Kristin et al., 'Kindness counts: Prompting prosocial behaviour in preadolescents boosts peer acceptance and well-being', *PLoS ONE*, vol. 7, no. 12, e51380.

12 Nyklíček, Ivan and Kuijpers, Karlijn F., 'Effects of mindfulness-based stress reduction intervention on psychological well-being and quality of life: Is increased mindfulness indeed the mechanism?', *Annals of Behavioral Medicine*, vol. 35, no. 3, pp. 331–40.

13 Raes, Filip et al., 'School-based prevention and reduction of depression in adolescents: A cluster-randomized controlled trial of a mindfulness group program', *Mindfulness*, vol. 5, no. 5, pp. 477–86.

14 Vibe, Michael de et al., 'Six-year positive effects of a mindfulness-based intervention on mindfulness, coping and well-being in medical and psychology students: Results from a randomized controlled trial', *PLoS ONE*, vol. 13, no. 4, e0196053.

15 'Causes of death, Australia, 2017: Intentional self-harm, key characteristics', Australian Bureau of Statistics, 26 September 2018.

16 All of these statistics are quoted in the Australian Government's report 'The mental health of children and adolescents: Report on the second Australian child and adolescent survey of mental health and wellbeing', Lawrence, David et al., August 2015.

CHAPTER 8: A FILE CALLED REGRET

1 '9 in 10 Aussie teens now have mobile (and most are already on their second or subsequent handset)', Roy Morgan, 22 August 2016.

2 'Australian Child Health Poll – Screen time and kids: What's happening in our homes?', The Royal Children's Hospital Melbourne, June 2017.

3 Ibid.

4 'Literature review: Impact of mobile digital devices in schools', Griffiths, Kate and Williams, Maddy, NSW Government Department of Education, December 2018.

5 'Mobile phones to be banned in state primary and secondary schools', *The Age*, 25 June 2019.

6 'Number of monthly active Facebook users worldwide as of 2nd quarter 2019 (in millions)', Clement, J., Statista, 9 August 2019.

7 Tristan Harris in conversation with Sam Harris on *Making Sense with Sam Harris*, podcast, 14 April 2017.

8 Ibid.

9 'Smart everything, everywhere: Mobile consumer survey 2017, the Australian cut', Deloitte, 2017.

10 Ibid.

11 'Gaming disorder', World Health Organization, September 2018.

CHAPTER 14: A QUICK WORD ON BUSINESS

1 World Health Organization, 'The global burden of disease', 2004 update, as cited in: 'Facts & figures about mental health', Black Dog Institute.

MENTAL HEALTH SUPPORT SERVICES

Adult

Lifeline: 13 11 14
lifeline.org.au

Suicide Call Back Service: 1300 659 467
suicidecallbackservice.org.au

Beyond Blue: 1300 22 4636
beyondblue.org.au

MensLine Australia: 1300 78 99 78
mensline.org.au

Youth

Kids Helpline: 1800 551 800
kidshelpline.com.au

headspace: 1800 650 890
headspace.org.au

ReachOut: au.reachout.com

Other resources

Life in Mind (suicide prevention portal):
lifeinmindaustralia.com.au

Head to Health (mental health portal):
headtohealth.gov.au

SANE (online forums): sane.org

GEM EXERCISES

GRATITUDE

What are three things that went well for you today?

1. _____

_____

_____

2. _____

_____

_____

3. _____

_____

_____

What are you looking forward to most about tomorrow?

_____

_____

_____

_____

_____

_____

_____

_____

EMPATHY

Think about someone you know who is going through or has gone through a tough time. What would you say to them? Draft a response below, then send them an email or text to let them know you're thinking of them.

_____

_____

_____

_____

_____

_____

_____

_____

_____

_____

_____

_____

_____

MINDFULNESS

**Go for a walk and think about three things you can see,
three things you can hear and three things you feel.
Write them down here.**

_____

_____

_____

_____

_____

_____

_____

_____

_____

_____

_____

_____

_____

Discover a
new favourite

Visit **penguin.com.au/readmore**